OXFORD
UNIVERSITY PRESS

ASPIRE
SUCCEED
PROGRESS

T0369571

Complete
English as a
Second Language
for Cambridge IGCSE®

Writing and Grammar Practice Book

Lucy Bowley
Alan Jenkins
Series editor: Dean Roberts

Oxford excellence for Cambridge IGCSE®

OXFORD

OXFORD
UNIVERSITY PRESS

Great Clarendon Street, Oxford, OX2 6DP, United Kingdom

Oxford University Press is a department of the University of Oxford. It furthers the University's objective of excellence in research, scholarship, and education by publishing worldwide. Oxford is a registered trade mark of Oxford University Press in the UK and in certain other countries

© Oxford University Press, 2017

The moral rights of the authors have been asserted

First published in 2017

All rights reserved. No part of this publication may be reproduced, stored in a retrieval system, or transmitted, in any form or by any means, without the prior permission in writing of Oxford University Press, or as expressly permitted by law, by licence or under terms agreed with the appropriate reprographics rights organization. Enquiries concerning reproduction outside the scope of the above should be sent to the Rights Department, Oxford University Press, at the address above.

You must not circulate this work in any other form and you must impose this same condition on any acquirer

British Library Cataloguing in Publication Data available

978-0-19-839608-6

10

Paper used in the production of this book is a natural, recyclable product made from wood grown in sustainable forests. The manufacturing process conforms to the environmental regulations of the country of origin.

Printed and bound by CPI Group (UK) Ltd, Croydon, CR0 4YY

Acknowledgements

The publisher would like to thank the following for permission to use their photographs:

Cover: Shutterstock; p4: Best View Stock/Alamy Stock Photo; p32: Arndt Sven-Erik/ Arterra Picture Library/Alamy Stock Photo; p46: Deepspace/Shutterstock; p83(tl): Kevin George/123RF; p83(tr): Sara Winter/123RF; p83(bl): Stevanzz/123RF; p88: iStockphoto; p102: Andrey Lobachev/Shutterstock; p116: Vacclav/123RF; p158: Robert Gilhooly/Alamy Stock Photo. All other images: Shutterstock

We are grateful to the authors and publishers for use of extracts from their titles and in particular for the following:

Alastair Humphreys: `A Bit of Background to "Into The Empty Quarter"' from http://www. alastairhumphreys.com/a-bit-of-background-to-into-the-empty-quarter. Reproduced by permission.

Extracts from Minack Theatre from https://www.minack.com/our-history-1/. Reproduced by permission of the Minack Theatre Trust.

Extract from Shanghai Science & Technology Museum Introduction from http://www.sstm. org.cn/kjg_Web/html/kjg_english2014/portal/index/index.htm. Reproduced by permission.

We have made every effort to trace and contact all copyright holders before publication, but if notified of any errors or omissions, the publisher will be happy to rectify these at the earliest opportunity.

Links to third party websites are provided by Oxford in good faith and for information only. Oxford disclaims any responsibility for the materials contained in any third party website referenced in this work.

® IGCSE is the registered trademark of Cambridge International Examinations.

All sample questions and answers within this publication have been written by the authors. In examination, the way marks are awarded may be different.

This Practice Book refers to the Cambridge IGCSE® English as a Second Language (Speaking endorsement) (0510) and Cambridge IGCSE® English as a Second Language (Count-in speaking) (0511) Syllabuses published by Cambridge Assessment International Education.

This work has been developed independently from and is not endorsed by or otherwise connected with Cambridge Assessment International Education.

The manufacturer's authorised representative in the EU for product safety is Oxford University Press España S.A. of el Parque Empresarial San Fernando de Henares, Avenida de Castilla, 2 – 28830 Madrid (www.oup.es/en).

Contents

Access your support website for answers:
www.oxfordsecondary.com/9780198396086.

Introduction

This Practice Book builds on the skills introduced in the Student Book to help you develop and improve your grammar and writing skills in the key areas that will also help you achieve success in the Cambridge IGCSE English as a Second Language examination.

Developing your knowledge and building new vocabulary

Each chapter starts with a short, interesting article to introduce you to the chapter theme followed by questions to check your understanding and develop your ability to analyse and evaluate. We take this opportunity to help you learn some new words – all of these have been chosen carefully as they could easily feature in articles you might see in your IGCSE Reading examination questions.

Developing your grammar

Each of the twelve chapters in this book covers three elements of grammar, which are linked to the theme of the chapter. You will find three different boxes to support you in your understanding of the grammar points:

- Remember – short reminders of key grammar skills that you should already know.
- Looking closely – introduces new grammar teaching, and explains how it is used.
- Teacher tips – hints or tips that try to bring out the main learning point and help you move forward.

This book offers task-based practice: for each grammar skill, we will help you build up your knowledge and invite you to write responses to exercises in order to refine and improve your grammar. We do not expect you to achieve perfection by this stage, so please do not think of this as an end-point. Rather, we hope it encourages you to practise more!

Developing your writing

The second half of each chapter can be thought of as a writing workshop, which aims to show you how twelve different styles of writing are constructed. In each unit, you will be asked to generate one piece of extended writing (around 200 words), each of which has a particular style, tone and audience. These include informal, semi-formal and formal registers.

The book goes further than these styles of writing, however, and aims to help you develop a broader range of writing skills. Therefore, you will also practise writing reviews, writing blogs, technical writing, writing a speech and some other forms of writing which are useful for success at IGCSE level.

The key features of each writing skill are covered as we help you build up to your final, 200-word piece. A range of "write-in" methods are used to check your understanding of each writing style. Then it's over to you to bring all of your new learning together into one piece of fluent and impressive writing!

Checking your progress

Each chapter ends with a short, fun quiz, focusing on the grammar skills you developed in the first part of the chapter and the writing skills you have been refining in the second part. The quiz also asks you to evaluate your own progress in a grammar and writing skills' checkpoint.

Checking your answers

Once you have completed a chapter, you can check your answers online (see Contents on page 2). For the writing tasks, we have provided some guidance to help you think about what a good answer would look like. However, you may also decide to ask your teacher to check your writing and make suggestions for where you could improve. Whatever you decide, the most important thing is for you to keep practising!

1 Science and technology

You are going to spend the day at the Shanghai Science & Technology Museum, where you can see a wide range of scientific inventions and modern technology. Look at the list of attractions you might go and see. Which one would you go and see first and why?

World of Robots **Home on Earth** **Space Navigation** **Human and Health** **Children's Science Land**

I'd go and see _____

because _____

Visiting the museum

Shanghai Science & Technology Museum opened to the public on December 18, 2001. …

With the theme of "Nature ·Mankind ·Technology", Shanghai Science & Technology Museum works for **promoting** scientific and cultural quality of the whole citizens … of Shanghai. Shanghai Science & Technology Museum serves for the purposes of education, research, leisure traveling, **cooperation**, communication, collection and production. We aim at providing visitors opportunities of gaining science technology knowledge and spirits.

Shanghai Science & Technology Museum currently has opened 14 thematic exhibition halls to the public. They are: World of Animals, **Spectrum** of Life, Spider Exhibition, Earth Exploration, Cradle of Designers, Children's Science Land, Light of Wisdom, Home on Earth, Information Era, World of Robots, Light of Exploration, Human and Health, Space **Navigation** … Apart from the above-listed, there are Chinese Ancient Science & Technology Gallery showing off Chinese **ancient** inventions and creations, Explorers' Gallery featuring Chinese and foreign **distinguished** explorers and Academicians Gallery showing off contemporary scientists of Shanghai.

Here are four special purpose theaters in Shanghai Science & Technology Museum. They are: IMAX 3D Theater, IMAX Dome Theater, IWERKS Theater and Space Theater, which **constitute** the largest science educational cinema in Asia with 10 000 annual filming times.

http://www.sstm.org.cn/kjg_web/html/kjg_english/About_Introduction/List/list_0.htm

Building your vocabulary

promoting: supporting and actively encouraging

cooperation: working together

spectrum: wide range

navigation: planning and finding a route

ancient: belonging to the very distant past

distinguished: very successful and commanding great respect

constitute: to account for or to add up to

1. Without looking back, write down which year the museum was opened to the public.

   ----

2. Underline the reasons this museum exists. Hint – only two are correct.

   a. To promote China as an independent country.

   b. To exhibit ancient artefacts.

   c. To show the spectrum of creatures inhabiting the planet.

   d. To prioritise distinguished explorers from China.

3. If you were the tour guide of a group interested in modern technology, which two rooms would *you* take the group to?

   ----

4. What does this museum offer the cinema goer?

   ----

5. Do you think this facility has been successful since it opened? Why or why not?

   ----

6. If you were given a million dollars to set up a museum what would that museum look like?

Linking words

Remember

Linking words allow you to join two ideas together and they help you to organise your work more clearly. Therefore, linking words improve the flow of your writing and make your writing easier to read.

1. Write down four linking words you often use.

   a. ---

   b. ---

   c. ---

   d. ---

2. Now read this short passage and underline the linking words you find.

   > That morning, Peter decided to go to work by bus rather than take his usual train because it was early so he wanted to go to the shop and buy his mother some flowers for her birthday and maybe see the owner again. He knew she was a musician as she always put her guitar in the corner of the shop during the day before her concerts in the evenings. He loved playing the guitar too and planned to talk about his favourite guitar music if she was there that day.

Looking closely

Linking words play different roles. For example, *and, but, because* link two ideas together. We use *and* when the ideas are similar, and *but* when the ideas are different, so we need to choose our words carefully. The word *because* is followed by a reason. Some linking words can appear at the start of a sentence and serve as connectors from the previous sentence: *also, secondly, next* are examples of linking words used for this purpose.

3. Fill in the gaps in the following paragraph with a linking word from the box. Note the particular purpose of each one as you do this.

   > as well as • which also then soon after

   Peter decided he wanted to go to a museum so he called his friend Zak who ------------- enjoyed science.

   They ------------- decided to go to the science centre, ------------- had only opened the previous weekend.

   ------------- Peter and Zak, there were several of their friends there and they all had a good look round together. ------------- they had finished, they went for some lunch before going home.

4. Suggest a suitable linking word or words for each of these sentences. If you need to, you can change the sentences slightly.

   a. David enjoys going to museums. He goes with people he doesn't even know.

   ----

b. Duncan and Mohammad go to the City Science Museum on Saturdays. They have lunch together.

----

c. Jan loves technology. Jan goes to the new Technology Centre. It is near her gym.

----

d. Sara has invented new things. Sara has technology lessons at her school.

----

5. In the following sentences, there are three ideas. You can link them using one or two linking words, into either one or two sentences. The first one is done as an example:

a. José and Javier like to go to school. They like science lessons. Their favourite subject is Physics.

José and Javier like to go to school. They like science lessons because their favourite subject is Physics.

b. James is studying space at school. A play about space is being performed in his local theatre. James decides to go and see the space play at the theatre.

----

c. Ika goes to see Max at the weekends. Max lives far away from Ika. Ika uses a modern computer to talk to Max during the week.

----

d. Hee Mok and Stephen want to learn how to drive a car. They like watching cars on television. They have been having lessons for three months.

----

e. Mandy and Karen go to a shop each week to buy items they can use in science experiments. Mandy likes mixing things. Karen takes the role of observing and writing down what happens.

Comparatives

Looking closely

When two or more things are linked, you may want to compare them. You can use a comparative when you want to compare two things. For example:

- James saw the *newer, brighter* star first.

With the adjectives above (*new, bright*), you can add the suffix *-er* to make the comparative. With other adjectives, you can use *more* and retain the adjective:

- The second book was *more interesting* than the first.

Of course, there are exceptions. These are called irregular forms. For example:

- His second version of his invention *was better* than the first version.

1. Change the adjectives in the brackets into the comparative:

   a. The student wanted the _____ tablet. (robust)

   b. The man needed to hire a _____ car. (efficient)

   c. Jake thought the photo of the planets was _____ than the picture of the planets. (magnificent)

2. Write a paragraph of around 80 words that uses comparatives. Think of it as a blog entry where you describe a visit to a planetarium. Underline all the comparatives you use. We have started the blog for you.

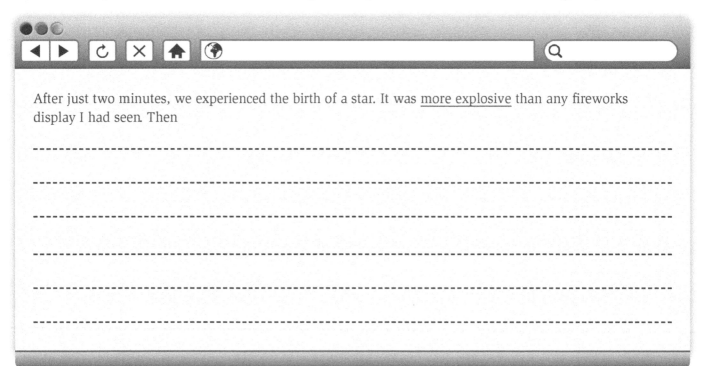

After just two minutes, we experienced the birth of a star. It was <u>more explosive</u> than any fireworks display I had seen. Then

_____

_____

_____

_____

_____

_____

Superlatives

Looking closely

You can use superlatives to compare three or more things or three stages of a process. This is usually done by using *the* and adding the suffix *-est*. These are called regular forms. For example:

- James thought *the newest* star shone *the brightest*.

In some cases, you can use *the* and *most* before the adjective. For example:

- *The most* popular subject this year was Technology.

Again, there are irregular forms that are exceptions to the rule. For example:

- The dual-fuel car went *the furthest* of all the cars tested.

3. Change the adjectives in brackets to a superlative to complete each sentence.

   a. Sam decided to buy -------------- telescope in the shop. (small)

   b. Abdul liked Chemistry, but liked Physics lessons -------------. (good)

   c. Pablo wanted to be ------------- scientist in the world. (fame)

4. Draw lines to match the sentence halves below.

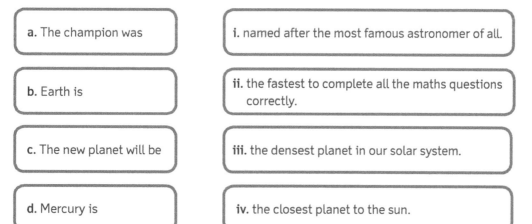

a. The champion was

i. named after the most famous astronomer of all.

b. Earth is

ii. the fastest to complete all the maths questions correctly.

c. The new planet will be

iii. the densest planet in our solar system.

d. Mercury is

iv. the closest planet to the sun.

5. Write a paragraph of around 80 words that uses superlatives. Create another blog entry where you describe a visit to a technology fair. Underline all the superlatives you use. We have started the blog for you.

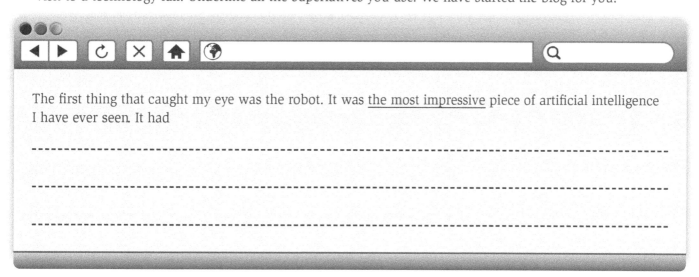

The first thing that caught my eye was the robot. It was <u>the most impressive</u> piece of artificial intelligence I have ever seen. It had

----

Present simple verb tense

Remember

The present simple tense is the base form of the verb: I *work* as a scientist in New York.
The third person (she/he/it) adds an -s: she *works* as a scientist in New York.

The present continuous tense is formed from the present tense of the verb *to be* and the present participle (*-ing*) of a verb: she *is* now *working* as a scientist in New York.

1. Complete these sentences using the present simple tense of a suitable verb.

   a. I often _____ by train up to the city.

   b. Juan _____ to go to the design and technology museum after school.

   c. She _____ to study more physics if she is going to pass the test.

   d. We _____ maths lessons every Monday morning.

   e. Mars _____ the closest planet to Earth.

Looking closely

You should use the present simple tense for things that happen all the time. For example:

- The planets *orbit* the sun.
- The sun *sets* in the west.

You should also use it for something that is done often.
For example:

- He *visits* the museum every Monday.

Also, you can use it to describe a timetable or a schedule, such as:

- We *start* with a talk, then we *conduct* a short meeting before we *attend* the exhibition.

2. Use the verbs given below. Using the present simple, add one verb to each sentence.

go	see	check	have	make

   a. I _____ my work every time I finish writing something.

   b. She _____ beautiful cards and sells them on the Internet.

   c. You _____ to science lessons every week.

   d. They _____ the trains passing their house every day.

   e. We _____ a meeting before school today in the chemistry lab.

Remember

The simple future tense has two different forms in English: *will* and *is going to*. Although the two forms can sometimes be used interchangeably, they often express two different meanings. However, both uses refer to a specific time in the future.

3. Now complete these sentences using the present simple. Try to be adventurous with the verbs you choose. In these cases you also have to supply a noun or two. Remember to stay with the science and technology theme.

   For example:

   Every week, I use my telescope (noun) to gaze (verb) at the solar system.

   a. Once a month, we (verb) ------------------------- a new (noun) ------------------------- in our

      science lessons.

   b. Annually, there is a (noun) ------------------------- and I (verb) ------------------------- it.

   c. My local (noun) ------------------------- has a technology park that seems (verb)

      ------------------------- all the time.

   d. On a Wednesday, I (verb) ------------------------- with my friends and we (verb)

      ------------------------- our (noun) -------------------------.

4. Read the following paragraph which uses the future tense to describe technology in the future. Then imagine that it's now the year 2020. Identify the verbs in the future tense and change them into the present simple.

   In 2020 we will have a hover-board that will allow us to move over the pavements instead of walking on them. The hover-board will be made of carbon fibre and is going to use air to propel it upwards. It is also going to contain electromagnets to force it away from the gravitational pull of the earth. While the prototype board will hover over land, the second planned board is going to be able to function over water.

   In 2020, we now have ......
   _____

   _____

   _____

   _____

   _____

   _____

   _____

Writing to persuade

Think about the best scientific or technological gadget you have bought.

- Why did you buy it?

- Did you buy it online? Where did you buy it from?

- How do you feel about your purchase?

I bought a _____

I bought it from _____

because _____

Since I have owned this gadget I feel _____

There are some occasions when _____

_____

I intend to _____

_____

1. We buy things sometimes because we need them and sometimes because we have been persuaded to, either by other people or by advertising. What words might persuade you to buy something? Look at these lines from adverts and underline all the language that is trying to persuade you to make the purchase.

   a. Now is the time to buy the number one microscope on the market. It's *Clear Vision*.

   b. Have to know all about the latest gadgets? Then you need to buy *Inventing Today*!

   c. You won't want to miss reading this month's edition of *The Night Sky* – it tells you exactly where to see Jupiter, and at its brightest on June 23rd.

   d. Need to pass a maths exam soon? Go and buy *The Easy Way to Maths* before you go home tonight to ensure success.

2. Write down four things you feel persuaded you to buy your gadget.

   a. _____

   b. _____

   c. _____

   d. _____

3. Look at these five sentences. Put them in order of how persuasive they are where 1 is the most persuasive and 5 is the least persuasive.

Number

a. I wouldn't buy that if I were you; I bought one and it broke the following week.

b. It is the best gadget I have ever bought. I would definitely recommend it.

c. While the product itself was very good I wouldn't buy it from this shop again as the assistant was very unhelpful.

d. I bought one last month and I like it. The price was reasonable and it does everything it claims to.

e. This is a very good product. I bought it as a replacement but really it is an upgrade as it does far more than my old one. My only problem was the price as it was a bit high.

4. a. Start an email to a friend describing a gadget you don't have but would really like to buy. Persuade your friend to buy one too. Write the opening two or three sentences.

----

b. Did you use any adjectives in your email? Underline any you used.

c. Think of three new or different adjectives you can add to make your opening lines even more persuasive. Say why you added these.

i. --

ii. --

iii. --

Describing a museum visit

1. a   Your class has free tickets for the Science Museum of London. Look it up on the Internet. What can you see at this museum? Think about the general areas of interest as well as specific exhibits that attract people to the museum. If you wanted to see one thing in the museum, what would it be?

   ----

   b. Museums are always updating their spaces and including new areas. Which of these might you see in a science museum in addition to the exhibits? Tick your choices.

interactive maps ☐	cinema ☐	crèche ☐
classroom mini zoo ☐	Jupiter ☐	library ☐
souvenir shops ☐	café ☐	gravity ☐
Stephen Hawking ☐	lift ☐	cloakroom ☐
escalator ☐	restaurant ☐	

Guidance

Different registers are used for different writing genres.

Formal register   We use formal language when writing to people we do not know and usually about something important, such as when writing a report.

Semi-formal register This is appropriate if you are writing to an audience you are aware of. You can use some idiomatic language, but not slang. For example, you could use semi-formal language in a school magazine.

Informal register   Use this to write to close friends about things you want to share with them. As you know your audience very well, you can use some slang and perhaps abbreviations that only the two of you know.

Planning

2. You have been chosen to write about a science trip for your school newspaper and you are going to write a semi-formal account about it here, persuading your audience that it is a worthwhile and valid experience. Start by choosing your science museum. Write its name here:

   ----

3. What is it about the museum trip that you would like to focus on? Tick three things from the list below.

    How did you get there, and how was the journey?

    What was your initial reaction when you arrived at the museum?

    What was the highlight of the day?

    What has been learned from the trip?

    Is there anything about the visit that should be changed if it is done again?

    Would you recommend the visit? Why or why not?

4. You are writing an account, so you need to use semi-formal language. Which of the following writing styles do you think would fit best in your descriptive account? Tick your choice.

    a. "Wow. You should have seen the interactive dinosaur. It blew our minds."

    b. "The stegosaurus had mechanical legs which utilised the principle of hydraulics to create the effect of movement. These were engineered using the Bowley-Roberts method of super-dynamics invented in pre-war Poland."

    c. "Almost everyone enjoyed seeing the life-size dinosaur move using its mechanical legs. The effect was very realistic and made some of us a little nervous."

Writing

5. You are now ready to write your own account to describe the day at the science museum. On a separate sheet of paper write your account of the day. Aim to write 150–200 words. Remember to only produce three paragraphs.

Skills checklist

When you have finished your account, complete the following checklist.

?   Have you written three paragraphs?

?   Have you described the day at the museum clearly?

?   Have you used persuasive language?

Checking your progress

1. When he walked on the moon, Neil Armstrong said: "This is one small step for a man, one giant leap for mankind." Write a quote that summarises your learning about science or technology.

Grammar

2. Below are some statements. Use any of the linking words you have used in this chapter to create two sentences with different meanings.

   - My favourite subject is science.
   - I enjoy my computer lessons.
   - I read about science in my free time.
   - I have been to my local science museum recently.

   a. _____

   b. _____

3. Which of these is a comparative sentence? Tick the correct sentence.

   a. My job as a research scientist pays me as much as when I was working in a shop! ☐

   b. I am the old one here, not you. ☐

   c. If you heat sulphuric acid it will create more havoc than you can handle. ☐

4. Draw lines to match the sentence halves to make three superlative sentences.

a. His maths test result	i. are the most interesting things in the sky.
b. The stars	ii. will be the most famous in the world.
c. My idea	iii. was the best in the class.

5. In the gaps below add five different verbs in the present tense.

   I _____ to school every day with Jake. He _____ going to physics classes and _____ a lot about inventing. Hannah _____ for a brand new phone and _____ to play games on it.

Writing

6. Which sentence would persuade you most to buy an item? Tick your choice.

    a. I am not sure about it, but a friend of a friend said it was pretty good. ◯

    b. I would buy it as it sounds fantastic. ◯

    c. The reviews gave it 4.5 stars out of 5 and that was based on nearly 200 reviews. ◯

7. Put these words or phrases in order, from 1 to 8, where 1 persuades you most.

| just wonderful ◯ | quite average ◯ | first class ◯ | I've seen better ◯ |
| not ideal but ◯ | isn't it lovely? ◯ | definitely the best ◯ | I've seen worse ◯ |

8. You are going to a museum. Which of these things would be most useful to have with you? Tick your choice.

    compass ◯   map of the museum ◯   sandwich ◯   pencil ◯

Now write a persuasive sentence to explain your choice.

----

9. For each of these terms write two words you associate with the subject.

    ● Science: ------------------------------- Information: -------------------------------

    ● Technology: ------------------------------- Nuclear: -------------------------------

10. Now it is time to make an evaluation of your progress through this chapter. Circle your response.

    a. How confident are you when:

● *Using comparatives?*	very	quite	sometimes	not very	I need help
● *Using superlatives?*	very	quite	sometimes	not very	I need help
● *Using persuasive writing?*	very	quite	sometimes	not very	I need help

    b. Write a phrase you have learned in this chapter that you can use to make your writing more persuasive.

----

    c. Write a question of your own for an area of grammar or writing discussed in this chapter, perhaps focusing on an area you struggle with. Choose any question format you like. Then have an answer ready and try the question out on someone you know.

Food and fitness

Think about what it would be like appearing on television. Would you like to appear on television? Why or why not?

I would love to appear on television because

Personally, I wouldn't enjoy appearing on television as it would be

----

Each summer on television, over ten weeks, there is a **reality show** called *The Great British Bake Off*, or *Bake Off* to its fans. It starts with 12 **contestants**, who are experienced bakers, and one loses their place on the show each week until the final three compete to see who is the winner. Contestants have to bake three things on each show. Two judges, Mary and Paul, decide who is the best and who is the worst. No-one wants to be **eliminated**, but this will happen to the worst performers.

Although it is called *The Great British Bake Off*, the bakers do not just bake British food. For example, Mary and Paul have challenged contestants to make baklava, strudel, cheesecake and eclairs. Sometimes, people are given detailed recipes to follow, and sometimes they are just given the ingredients and the name of what they are making. Occasionally, they have to bake without really knowing what the end product is supposed to look like. Everything is done **against the clock**, so the contestants are really **under pressure**. They have to bake everything correctly, but they lose marks if they do not finish on time.

Even the most relaxed cooks can **end up** feeling quite tense during the competition. Some bakes have even ended up in the bin, rather than on a plate. Mel and Sue help the contestants along the way and the thought of being the best cook on the programme keeps contestants going, but it is Mary and Paul who decide who stays in the competition and who will be going home each week.

Building your vocabulary

reality show: a television programme or series showing people in real situations

contestants: people in a competition

eliminated: knocked out of the competition and asked to leave

against the clock: with a time limit

under pressure: with a feeling of having to perform well, not relaxed

end up: finish

1. Who judges the competition? Underline your answer.

   a. The viewers

   b. Mary and Paul

   c. Mel and Sue

2. Why are the contestants under pressure? Underline your answer.

   a. There is a time limit.

   b. They don't have all the ingredients.

   c. They haven't baked before.

3. What happens each week to the contestant who is the worst baker?

   ----

4. In your view, why is it more exciting to watch something when the contestants have to complete it against the clock?

   ----

5. Find two examples of strong descriptive words or phrases in the text.

   ----

6. If you were on this show, what would you bake? Is it something you have baked before and if so, when was the last time you made it and why? Write only two sentences.

Collocations

Looking closely

Collocations are words regularly used together and there is usually no surprise to see such words paired. For example, *high-tech gadgets* and *reflective clothing* are collocations.

The collocations have been underlined in this review of some latest sports equipment:

- This is the latest <u>high-end range</u> from the maker of sportswear, B & D. They have produced some <u>ultramodern styles</u> combined with the latest <u>cyber engineering</u> to cater for the growing demand in the teenage market.

1. Look at what you are wearing or objects you can see and think which collocations could go with those items. You can choose words other than the ones given above. For example, trousers could become *beautifully cut* trousers or *freshly ironed* trousers.

   Write down four things you are wearing or can see, together with their collocations.

   a. _____

   b. _____

   c. _____

   d. _____

2. Make your own collocations by drawing lines between words from list A and words from list B. Then, use each one in a sentence of your choice.

A	B
tear-resistant	trainers
fully contoured	jacket
high-energy	watch
16GB	snack

   _____

   _____

   _____

   _____

   _____

   _____

   _____

Looking closely

Here are a few more collocations that work with the nouns from exercise 2:

- *hard-wearing trainers*
- *high-visibility jacket*
- *water-resistant watch*
- *home-made snack.*

Yes, you can also have water-resistant trainers and a water-resistant jacket!

3. Now you have some examples to use to fill in the gaps in the paragraph below. Also think some of your own and complete the paragraph.

> When I have my birthday, I always update my fitness wardrobe. This year, I have bought some _____
>
> trainers and a _____ jacket, as well as a _____ watch. I take a _____ snack to my fitness
>
> class, which I eat afterwards.

Remember

Collocations go with certain nouns, but might go together with more than one. You can have a *lightweight sports jacket* and a *lightweight pair of trainers*. Collocations often evoke at least one of the senses when used with food. Examples are: *aromatic* long-grain rice; *tasty* freshly made bread.

4. Pick a collocation from the box to complete the paragraph below.

> lightweight   in-built   off the scale   cutting edge   self-tie

> Today we are reviewing the latest in running shoes. These ones use the latest _____ technology
>
> and _____ materials. We like the _____ mini-computer that tracks your every movement
>
> as well as the _____ laces, which come in some cool colours. The _____ price is not
>
> great though, so I think we will be buying a cheaper pair than this one.

Adjectives

Remember

Adjectives add detail to the nouns they are describing. They help the writer give a more detailed picture to the reader than would be possible using just the nouns on their own. Adjectives can be used to describe the shape, colour, number, quality, age and origin of the noun.

1. Many communities have annual food festivals, part of which often involves a cooking competition. What might a judge want a cake to be like? Tick three of the words on the list below.

   fluffy ☐   crispy ☐

   underdone ☐   moist ☐

   creamy ☐

2. You might make a pie or some jam for a cooking competition. Add three more adjectives to each list. There is an example for each one provided for you.

PIE	JAM
well-filled	sweet

3. You have cooked something to enter into a food competition. Write three sentences to describe what it is. Make sure you have used adjectives to make it sound attractive and appetising. Underline the adjectives afterwards.

   a. _____

   b. _____

   c. _____

4. Unfortunately, your friend did not do as well as expected in the competition. Write three more sentences to describe your friend's entry, and at the end explain why it did not win.

   a. _____

   b. _____

   c. _____

   d. My friend did not win because _____

   _____

Keeping fit

5. After eating all of this food, we might find ourselves needing to improve our fitness. How do you keep fit? Why is it important?

I keep fit by:

a. --

b. --

c. --

I think it's important to stay fit because it:

d. --

e. --

f. --

6. Find six adjectives in the wordsearch that relate to fitness. The first letter of each of the six words has been highlighted for you.

M	O	T	I	V	A	T	I	N	G
H	E	C	U	L	A	R	B	L	E
E	N	M	O	T	S	L	A	R	N
A	E	N	E	F	I	C	I	A	L
L	R	O	A	A	E	H	C	E	E
T	G	Y	R	R	C	T	T	Y	N
H	E	N	J	O	Y	A	B	L	E
Y	T	B	L	N	E	I	E	G	U
A	I	L	N	M	T	G	H	U	T
M	C	M	U	S	C	U	L	A	R
B	E	N	E	F	I	C	I	A	L

7. Now insert one of the adjectives you found in the wordsearch into each of the sentences below.

a. I like my spin class but it is very _____.

b. Sam likes to follow a _____ lifestyle.

c. I am getting fitter and I find it _____.

d. Since joining the gym, Max has become more _____.

e. We have joined an _____ tennis class.

f. They see that doing more exercise is _____.

Past simple verb tense

Looking closely

The past simple is used to denote something that happened in the past, for example:

- I saw a great film.

To create the past simple verb tense, *-ed* is usually added to the main verb stem. For example:

- Jake *chopped* the carrots to add to the pot.
- Ash *prepared* a casserole for the competition.

Now here are some alternatives to these verbs:

- Jake *dug* his own carrots to add to the pot, while Ash *found* time to consult his cookbook.

What did you notice about these two words? Yes, they do not add *-ed* and that is because they are **irregular verbs**, which means they don't follow the usual pattern.

Here are some more:

- I *saw* a great recipe and so *went* to my local supermarket and *bought* all the ingredients.

1. Add verbs to complete this paragraph about a visit to a game. Use the past simple verb of your choice.

I _____ to the stadium and _____ the match. We _____

the tickets online before the game. Afterwards, we _____ some photos of the players.

I _____ the photos onto my social media page. Hundreds of people have now

_____ my photos.

Remember

A time marker can also be used to provide more information and can be placed before or after the main clause.

2. Think of some suitable past tense verbs to use in the sentences below and add a suitable time marker from the box. Take note of whether you use the regular or irregular verb form.

yesterday	last Sunday	last week
just now	a few minutes ago	last month

a. I _____ a cake and _____ it into a competition _____.

b. I finally _____ the television sports programme my friend _____ to me

_____.

c. _____ I _____ the fitness gadget you _____.

d. Juan -------------------- his brother to a football match -------------------- for his birthday.

e. -------------------- Stephanie -------------------- to walk 5 kilometres a day to get fitter but she -------------------- .

3. Change these verbs into the irregular past simple to complete the paragraph.

> Josh -------------- (go) to school and -------------- (see) his friends. They -------------- (swim)
>
> in the school swimming pool before they -------------- (eat) some lunch together. After school, they
>
> -------------- (make) a kite together which they then -------------- (fly) in the park opposite the school.

Looking closely

Looking at some of the sentences in this spread it would seem that alternative verbs can be used. For example:

- I *made* a cake and put it into the competition.

This could become:

- I *created* a cake and entered it into the competition.

However, sometimes the first verb you thought of is actually the best verb. For example:

- We *booked* the tickets online.

Booked tickets goes together well and you wouldn't need to change that, but what about:

- I *went* to the stadium and saw the match.

Here are some suggested alternatives:

- I *travelled* to the stadium and enjoyed the match.
- I *cycled* to the stadium and watched the match.

Try to make sure whatever verbs you use, you are also showing a range of them in your writing. Try to avoid repeating the same verb in a longer piece of writing.

Teacher tip

Sometimes you will be writing under time pressure and will need to choose a simple verb so your writing flow is not interrupted. However, you should ideally show the reader you have a range of language in your writing. You still need to plan enough time to proofread your sentences to make sure your language shows a good range.

Writing to avoid redundancy

Guidance

Your written work needs to avoid redundancy so that the overall flow of your writing is clear and smooth. For example, if there are too many repeated words in your writing, the reader will begin to lose interest.

Read this short paragraph, which uses too much repetition.

> I went to the stadium. I saw a football match at the stadium. I went with my friends. My friends and myself had a good time and we all had a good chat. The game was good. There is another football game next week in the stadium.

It doesn't quite flow does it?

Redundancy can simply be using words that do not need to be used. Redundant words can be any part of speech, but two common parts of speech where redundancy is found are nouns and verbs.

● I went to the stadium. I went with my friends could become…

   I went to the stadium *with my friends*.

● The *match* was good and there is another *match* next week could become…

   The match was good and there is another one next week.

It is always better to avoid repeating the same word where there is no need to do so.

1. Here is an email written by one friend to another. See if you can cross out the words or phrases that are not needed, but make sure you don't cross out any important information.

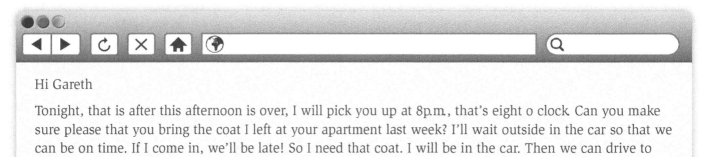

Hi Gareth

Tonight, that is after this afternoon is over, I will pick you up at 8p.m., that's eight o clock. Can you make sure please that you bring the coat I left at your apartment last week? I'll wait outside in the car so that we can be on time. If I come in, we'll be late! So I need that coat. I will be in the car. Then we can drive to the restaurant. I will park the car when we get there. We can both get out of the car. We can leave the car in the car park. We can then walk to the door of the restaurant. We can open that door. We can sit down. We can then eat. I'm really looking forward to seeing you again.

2. Rewrite the paragraph from the Guidance section above to make it smoother, clearer and more interesting for the reader.

   I went to the stadium…

   ----

3. To avoid redundancy in your writing, make sure you have linked the parts about the same idea rather than repeating the idea. Here is the follow-on paragraph about the same football match. Unfortunately, the writer has not proofread the work and there is some redundancy. Read it and underline the parts you think are redundant.

> I will take Bob and Fred with me next time. Bob and Fred are my friends. Bob and Fred love football. Bob and Fred like the same football team as me. After the match, I will take Bob and Fred to the new café at the stadium and in the café I will buy them a cup of coffee and a slice of cake.

4. Rewrite the paragraph, leaving out the redundant parts.

----

5. Add four more sentences to continue the paragraph, remembering what you have learned about redundancy and how to avoid it.

Writing a letter to a friend

Planning

1. You and your friends are excited to be going to a new sports club, which has recently opened near you. What is the new sports centre called?

   Write it here: _____

2. What facilities do you expect to find there? Complete the list below.

   a. Swimming pool

   b. _____

   c. _____

   d. _____

   e. _____

3. If you find a good sports centre, you will probably want to tell a friend about it, but what are the reasons why you want to go to the sports centre with your friend? Complete the notes below.

   - It is useful to go with a friend because then I can...

     _____

   - When we travel together it means we can...

     _____

   - The best thing about playing sport with a friend is...

     _____

4. You are going to write a letter telling a friend about your visit to the new sports centre in your area. Tick three things from the list below about the visit to the sports centre you would like to focus on.

   - The location of the sports centre.

   - The facilities the sports centre offers.

   - The value in terms of the prices the sports centre charges.

   - The classes which are offered at the sports centre.

   - The quality of the instructors at the sports centre.

   - What else there is to do there other than exercise in the sports centre.

5. Once you have finished your letter, you should check if there is any redundancy, so let's practise this. Read the paragraph below on the cost of going to the sports centre, underline redundant words and then rewrite it avoiding redundancy.

> The best thing about going together is that we will pay less than going on our own. The first person pays full price and the second person pays half the full price. I think that is really great and I think we need to go together, so we will pay less.

Writing

6. Now on a separate sheet of paper write your letter telling a friend about your visit to the new sports centre. Aim to write 150–200 words and use three paragraphs to cover the three areas you have chosen from the list in exercise 4.

Skills checklist

When you have finished your letter, complete the following checklist.

? Have you used an informal register?

? Did you include appropriate salutations?

? Have you found any redundant words?

? Could you have written fewer or longer sentences?

? Did you vary the use of verbs?

? Is there any information that doesn't need to be there?

Checking your progress

1. "We do not stop exercising because we grow old – we grow old because we stop exercising" Dr Kenneth Cooper, fitness expert, doctor and former soldier.

   Write a quote that summarises what you have learned about food or fitness.

Grammar

2. Add a food to each term below to make a collocation.

   a. Long-grain ---

   b. Freshly peeled ---

   c. Thinly cut ---

   d. Newly ground ---

   e. Ready-made ---

3. Draw lines to match these foods to their adjectives.

a. runny	i. meat
b. succulent	ii. lemon
c. bitter	iii. honey
d. soft	iv. nuts
e. crunchy	v. butter

4. If you wanted to recommend a cake to someone, which of these adjectives would you use? Tick your answer.

   a. crunchy

   b. moist

   c. dry

5. Add some past simple verbs to complete the sentences below.

   Last week, I ------------------- to the gym where I ------------------- a new fitness class. It

   ------------------- really fun and so I ------------------- the money for next week's class before I

   ------------------- home.

Writing

6. Cross out the redundant words in this passage, making sure you are maintaining the interest for the reader. Then rewrite the passage below.

> I have a younger brother. My younger brother's name is Daniel. Daniel likes to go swimming every week. Daniel has a certificate for his swimming. Daniel has put his swimming certificate on the wall of his bedroom. Daniel likes to look at the swimming certificate in his bedroom before he goes to sleep each night.

----

7. Put these sentences in the order the events happened. Use the number 1 for what happened first and 4 for what happened last. Write the numbers in the boxes.

a. I saw my friend on the treadmill.　　□　　**c.** So I put on my new trainers.　　□

b. I decided to go to the gym yesterday.　　□　　**d.** We had a coffee in the café afterwards.　　□

8. You have bought yourself a new gym bag. Write down two things you will need to put in it. You already have trainers packed.

a. ---

b. ---

9. Cross out any unnecessary words and then rewrite the paragraph below.

> I love going to the gym. When I go to the gym I often try out new equipment. The new equipment I tried out last time I went was a new sauna. It was very relaxing.

----

10. a. What have you learned in this chapter that should make your writing smoother and easier to read?

----

b. Make up a question about **collocations** and ask someone to answer it. It will be interesting to see whether the person gets the right answer.

----

3 Communities

Imagine you have been chosen to represent your school at a conference to discuss climate change and its potential effects on communities around the world. You will have to travel to the Arctic Circle to take part. Look at the list of challenges you may face in such an environment. Which one would be of most concern to you and why?

> freezing cold weather   polar bears   ice and snow   remote location

I would be most concerned by the

----

because

Arctic communities

The Arctic is a huge territory populated by **diverse** communities scattered throughout what is mostly remote and unyielding wilderness, where the temperature can fall to -30 degrees Celsius. Approximately 13 million people live in the vast expanse surrounding the Arctic Circle, known as the circumpolar north. Counted among these are a number of **indigenous** tribes, including the Inuit who founded the small town of Uummannaq on Greenland's northwest coast about 250 years ago.

In common with many of the other small communities dotted across this **inhospitable** landscape, Uummannaq is facing an uncertain future. In part, this is because of an ageing population and a desire within the younger generation to find economic **stability** elsewhere. But mainly it is because of the increasingly dramatic challenges caused by climate change. Both mainstays of the town's economy have become more dangerous and less productive because of the changing climatic conditions. Thinner ice has made **traversing** traditional hunting grounds on dog sleds much more **hazardous** during the winter months, but because the ice now begins to thaw earlier there is a period in the spring when the smaller fishing boats traditionally used by the Inuits cannot operate safely. Fishermen who are desperate to provide for their families cannot always do so.

Building your vocabulary

diverse: of several different kinds

indigenous: having always lived in a particular area

inhospitable: unfriendly and giving no shelter

stability: the state of being steady

traversing: to travel across something – on a journey

hazardous: dangerous or risky

1. Without referring to the text, write down how cold it can get in the Arctic Circle.

   ----

2. Tick the two reasons why Uummannaq is facing an uncertain future.

   a. It is situated in a cold and inhospitable part of the world. ☐

   b. The younger inhabitants are leaving to find better lives elsewhere. ☐

   c. The Arctic region is vast and Uummannaq is a small town. ☐

   d. Climate change has affected the Inuits' ability to hunt and fish properly. ☐

3. If you were traversing the area around Uummannaq on a dog sled, what might you see on your journey?

   ----

4. In your view, why has it become more hazardous for Inuit hunters since the climate has changed in the Arctic Circle?

   ----

5. In your view, why might having such a diverse population lead to difficulties for the inhabitants of the Arctic Circle to overcome the problems they face?

   ----

6. You have been asked to speak about the impact of climate change on Arctic communities. What would be the most important point you would make about climate change?

Collective nouns

Looking closely

A collective noun is the name given to people, animals, places and things when they are grouped together. Using the correct collective noun for each group makes the writing more precise and allows the reader a clearer idea of what the writer intended, rather than using a more general term such as *group*.

Here are some examples of collective nouns:

- Several people involved in a common activity can be referred to as a *crowd* of people.
- A number of birds flying together can be referred to as a *flock* of birds.
- People living together in a community of houses live on a housing *estate*.
- A number of storage crates placed on top of each other is a *stack* of crates.
- A group of wolves running together is referred to as a *pack*.

1. Place these collective nouns into the correct category box below. Some will fit into more than one category.

> team   set   class   fleet   chain   colony   constellation
> litter   tribe   jury   gang   city

People	Animals
Places	**Things**

2. Some nouns can be used in more than one category. For example, you can have a *tribe of people*, but you can also have a *tribe of monkeys*. Choose another word that fits into more than one box, and write two sentences using the same word in two different categories.

----

3. Choose a collective noun from the box for each of the groups.

> pod   team   party   crew

    a. The sailors who work on a fishing boat are called the _____.

    b. Huskies work in a _____ to pull a sled.

    c. When out fishing the sailors might see a _____ of whales.

    d. A _____ of tourists can sometimes be seen on Arctic cruises.

4. Read this passage and underline the collective nouns you find.

> The class of children watched with excitement as the fleet of fishing trawlers slowly exited the harbour in search of the shoal of fish that would be their catch. They talked with loud voices about what the fishermen might encounter on their voyage. Would there be a herd of reindeer, a flock of Canada geese, a colony of gulls or maybe even a pod of killer whales? They crowded around their teacher like a swarm of bees in eager anticipation of her thoughts in response to their questions.

Looking closely

To build a sentence using a collective noun, you will also need to consider using a verb and a pronoun. A verb describes an action, process, feeling or state while a pronoun replaces the noun or noun phrase in a sentence or clause to add variety to the writing.

An example is: *The pod of whales swims to its hunting grounds.* (Here *pod* is the collective noun used to describe the whales, *swims* is the verb in singular form and *its* is the pronoun also in singular form.)

5. These sentences contain collective nouns, but incorrectly use verbs and pronouns in plural form. Write them in their correct form.

    a. A herd of reindeer run when they are threatened.

    _____

    b. A flock of geese fly to their feeding grounds.

    _____

    c. The Inuit tribe hunt in the Arctic as it is their tradition to do so.

    _____

    d. Uummannaq's council vote to decide their policies at their meetings.

    _____

Active and passive verbs

Remember

Verbs can be active or passive depending on the purpose of the sentence. Both forms are grammatically correct, but it is important to know when to use one rather than the other. The majority of sentences you will encounter contain active verbs as this is the most straightforward way of communicating an idea.

Looking closely

Let's focus on active verbs. This is an example of an active sentence using an active verb.

A polar bear mother   nurtures   her cubs.

   (subject)   (active verb)   (object)

In this sentence the subject comes before the verb and the object follows it. This is because the subject is doing the action and the object is receiving the action.

1. Here is another active sentence. Identify the subject, verb and object.

   Inuit elders teach their young to hunt.

   Subject: _____

   Active verb: _____

   Object: _____

2. When you use an active sentence the subject always appears before the verb and the object always appears after it. Look at these sentences and underline the active verb in each one.

   a. Arctic communities share news.

   b. Communities cooperate frequently.

   c. Fishermen sail in all kinds of weather.

3. Match these subjects, active verbs and objects to make five active sentences.

Subject	Active verb	Object
Hunters	live in	dangerous seas.
Tourists	roam	the Arctic Circle.
13 million people	appreciate	the Arctic waters.
Whales	navigate	food.
Fishing trawlers	provide	Arctic wildlife.

   (Subject + Active verb + Object)

   a. _____

   b. _____

   c. _____

   d. _____

   e. _____

Passive verbs

Looking closely

The passive form is used when the object receiving the action becomes the subject because it is considered more important than what is doing the action.

For example: *Cubs are nurtured by their polar bear mothers.*

In this sentence the cubs are emphasised by placing them first even though it is the mother who is doing the action. The verb *nurtured* is in past participle form, which is typical of passive verb usage.

Another example is: *The Inuits' ability to hunt is adversely affected by unusual climatic conditions.*

You can also use the passive form when you are not certain who is doing the action.

4. Change these active sentences into passive form.

a. Arctic communities use satellites to predict the weather.

----

b. Inuit women prepare the fish.

----

c. Arctic communities enjoy diverse cultures.

----

d. The tourist industry employs many ex-fishermen.

----

e. Uummannaq trawlers travel hundreds of miles to catch fish.

Teacher tip

The passive form is often used in more formal writing when the action is deemed more important than the subject. Reports of an official nature or scientific studies are examples of when the passive form is considered more appropriate.

Suffixes and comparative adjectives

Looking closely

A suffix is added to the end of the word. Suffixes can be used to create comparisons. For example:

Here is an example: Arctic communities are *smaller* than most European cities.

By adding the suffix *–er* to the adjective *small* the size of the respective communities is compared.

Comparisons can also be made by placing the word *more* in front of the adjective, as in:

- The icy polar wind is *more* dangerous than the warm Saharan wind.

By placing *more* before the adjective a comparison is made between the winds in the two areas.

When do you use *–er, r* or *more*? As a general rule you use *–er* for shorter words and *more* for longer ones, but there are exceptions. For example:

- Sunlight in the desert is *more intense* than in the Arctic.

In this example, *intense* already ends in the letter e, so adding *–er* would make it *intenseer* which sounds wrong and is incorrect.

1. Using the suffix *–er*, add the correct form of the adjective to create the comparison. The first one is done for you.

   a. The Arctic is cold in the autumn months, but colder in the winter.

   b. Uummannaq is old, but Istanbul is ------------------.

   c. Polar bears are strong swimmers, but seals are ------------------.

   d. The North Star is bright, but the Northern Lights are ------------------.

2. Now complete these examples to create the comparison.

   a. Alsatians are powerful, but huskies are ------------------ ------------------.

   b. Fishing trawlers are resilient, but icebreakers are ------------------ ------------------.

   c. I think arctic wolves are frightening, but bears are ------------------ ------------------.

   d. Sudden storms are a constant threat, but thin ice is a ------------------ ------------------ threat.

3. Use either the suffix *–er* or *more* to compare each one of these pairs in a sentence. The first one is completed for you as an example.

   Uummannaq   New York City

   wolves   domestic animals

   blizzards   rain showers

   a. The crime rate in New York City is **higher** than in Uummannaq.

   b. --

   c. --

Superlative adjectives

Looking closely

The comparative degree formed by adding the suffix –er to a word or using *more* before the adjective is used to compare two things. If more than two are being compared then the adjective should take the form of a superlative. The suffix –est is added to the adjective to create the superlative form, as in:

- The Arctic is cold, but the record for the *coldest* place on Earth belongs to Antarctica.

Not all comparative and superlative adjectives follow a regular form. Some are irregular. For example: *little* becomes *less* in the comparative form and *least* in the superlative.

4. Here are some more superlative adjectives. Write a sentence for each one.

> **a.** highest   **b.** longest   **c.** weakest   **d.** darkest

a. _____

b. _____

c. _____

d. _____

5. Think of other superlative adjectives and write them here.

_____ _____ _____ _____ _____ _____

6. Superlative adjectives are also formed by placing *most* before the adjective. Underline the superlatives in the following passage. There are six to find.

> It snows most densely near the North Pole when the winds are at their most ferocious and visibility is at
>
> its most limited. Any journey is at its most hazardous in these the most treacherous conditions man can
>
> encounter. The most knowledgeable inhabitants shut their doors and stay inside.

7. Complete the following table of irregular forms. The first is done for you.

	Comparative	Superlative
little hope	less hope	least hope
bad weather		
good conditions		

Writing a summary

Guidance

Writing a summary requires careful planning. A good summary is a shortened overview of the facts in a main text, which includes all the most important ideas in the order they appear in that text. Details and quotations are not needed as there is normally a word limit. The summary will be written in the writer's own words and not simply copied from the main text.

Register is the style chosen based on the reason for the summary – its purpose – and the target audience. In a summary the register should be formal and measured to reflect its purpose, which is to succinctly convey a series of facts based on the most important ideas in the text being summarised.

1. Complete the boxes to give you a checklist of how to write a summary correctly and how to avoid some basic errors.

Do:

- consider the _____ of the summary – what is it doing?
- consider the target _____
- _____ an appropriate register
- _____ to any given word limit
- make _____ word count
- paraphrase key _____
- sequence points logically in the _____ _____ as the original text
- use _____ spelling and sentence construction
- write in _____ constructed paragraphs
- use _____ words/phrases to create a natural flow

Do not:

- _____ any given word limit
- copy from the _____
- _____ the original meaning
- try to cover _____ in the text
- use _____ details or statistics
- _____ ideas and points
- use quotations from the _____
- use lists of points that _____ flow naturally
- write an introduction that _____ words and has little _____

2. Tick which of these sentences is written in the most appropriate register for a summary.

   a. Polar bears are awesome creatures that will bite your head off without thinking twice.

   b. Polar bears are amazing and probably the most dangerous predator on the planet.

   c. Polar bears are violent, dangerous predators.

3. Placing your points in the same order as in the text being summarised is important. The original text will have been written in a logical sequence that creates a natural flow, so the summary should mimic this. The following passage has been poorly written. Reorder it into a more logical sequence. To get you started, the opening sentence is given as sentence **a**. You may find it helpful to write out the sentences on another sheet of paper.

    a. Trust and cooperation are vital ingredients in any successful community.

    b. You are one of only 30 people living in an isolated community a day's drive from your nearest neighbouring town.

    c. You have to trust your neighbour to cooperate to drive you to the nearest hospital 300 miles away.

    d. Without trust there is little hope for the community's survival when things get tough.

    e. You suffer a medical emergency, but you don't have a 4x4 with snow treads and the weather has made the terrain treacherous.

    f. Without cooperation there is a significant increase in the danger from potential risks a community may face.

    g. Consider this scenario:

Your answer:

1st. = a

2nd. = _____   3rd. = _____

4th = _____   5th. = _____

6th = _____   7th. = _____

4. A summary should not be a list of points, but a piece of writing that flows. Using carefully chosen connectives and connecting phrases can help this process by combining more than one point into a sentence. Insert a suitable connective or connecting phrase from the box to complete these sentences.

> resulting in   however   because   yet   as opposed to   while

    a. Arctic winters can be treacherous _____ still the fishing fleet sails when it can.

    b. Searching for thin ice _____ controlling a dog sled takes great skill.

    c. Fishing by sled _____ fishing from a trawler is sometimes the only option in winter.

    d. Maintaining telecommunications is vital _____ Arctic communities are spread over hundreds of miles _____ major problems if they become isolated.

    e. Sunny winter days are welcome _____ the threat of an Arctic storm is ever present.

Your summary

Planning

Imagine you have been given a text about the problems faced by remote communities. Your task is to write a short summary outlining these problems.

1. Look at this opening paragraph from the text you have been given. Then using the 'Do' and 'Do not' boxes on page 40 to guide you, consider which of the following points should be included in your summary. Put a tick by those you feel are relevant.

> Communities that live in remote areas of the planet find it much harder to survive and thrive than those that are situated in more densely populated areas. Vital telecommunications are often disrupted by severe meteorological conditions, difficult terrain and the long distances involved between communities. It takes a special kind of people to overcome all the hardship they are forced to endure, especially when 70 per cent of 18 to 25-year-olds leave in search of higher wages in Northern Europe and do not return. Those who are left are often the less educated and less skilled. This in itself adds to the problem of sustaining the community.

a. Living in a place far away from other communities is really hard.

b. Being able to sustain important communication links is adversely affected by the weather, the landscape and how far away communities are from each other.

c. A particular kind of person is needed to survive.

d. Almost three quarters of the young people leave home.

e. The people who remain have limited skills.

2. Here is your summary of the first paragraph:

> Being able to sustain important communication links is adversely affected by the weather, the landscape and how far away communities are from each other. Almost three quarters of the young people leave home. The people who remain have limited skills.

When reading your summary which of these judgments do you think are valid? Tick all that apply.

a. The main points are covered.

b. It is paraphrased not copied.

c. It is in sequence.

d. It doesn't flow naturally.

e. It needs some rewording and more connectives.

3. Which of these is the most effective opening sentence for your summary? Tick your choice.

    a. The biggest problem is being able to sustain important communication links is adversely affected by the weather, the landscape and how far away communities are from each other. ☐

    b. One problem faced is being able to sustain important communication links which are adversely affected by the weather, the landscape and how far away communities are from each other. ☐

4. The remaining two sentences of the summary in the first paragraph can be linked to improve the flow. Choose the most effective alternative by underlining it.

    a. Almost three quarters of the young people leave home and the people who remain have limited skills.

    b. Another problem is that almost three quarters of the young people leave home but the people who remain have limited skills.

    c. A further issue is that almost three quarters of the young people leave home while those who remain have limited skills.

Writing

5. Here is the second paragraph of the text. On a separate sheet of paper write your summary.

> Arctic communities have always battled problems particular to the harsh climate, but recently these problems have become more severe. Climate change caused by global warming has drastically altered the hunting and fishing patterns that form the lifeblood of these settlements. Thin ice across traditional hunting and fishing grounds has led to extremely hazardous conditions for these hardy people. Using dog sleds to navigate areas where the thickness of the ice is no longer trustworthy has become dangerous to both man and dog, leading to a sharp downturn in the amount of fish caught and game hunted. This scarcity of food has led many families to go hungry during the terrible winter months when survival is already difficult enough.

Skills checklist

When you have finished your summary, complete the following checklist.

? Have you used an appropriate register? ☐

? Have you made every word count? ☐

? Have you paraphrased not copied? ☐

? Have you sequenced your points logically? ☐

? Have you used accurate spelling and punctuation? ☐

? Have you used appropriate connecting words and phrases to create a natural flow? ☐

Checking your progress

1. Nelson Mandela said this about the importance of community: *"A fundamental concern for others in our individual and community lives would go a long way in making the world the better place we so passionately dreamt of."* Write a quote that summarises why you think a sense of community is important.

Grammar

2. Draw lines to match the appropriate collective noun to the group.

a. Canada geese	i. government
b. Fishing boats	ii. crew
c. Members of a ship	iii. quartet
d. Those who rule the country	iv. flock
e. Four folk singers	v. fleet

3. Which of these sentences uses an active verb and which uses the passive form? Underline the verb and put **A** for active or **P** for passive by the side to show your answers.

	A or P
a. A fisherman sails in all kinds of weather.	
b. The workers on a fishing trawler are led by their captain.	

4. Which of these sentences uses a suffix to create a comparative? Tick the correct sentence.

   a. The Arctic Circle is a lonely place to live in winter.

   b. The European red fox is heavier than its Arctic cousin.

   c. The Arctic Circle and Antarctica both have Polar Regions.

5. Add a superlative adjective to each of these sentences.

   a. The Inuits are the ------------------ indigenous people living in the Arctic region.

   b. The ------------------ iceberg known to have existed in the North Atlantic rose 168 metres above sea level.

Writing

6. When asked to summarise what is important to Uummannaq's economy, which of these sentences is the most appropriate? Tick your answer.

a. The small coastal community of Uummannaq – population approximately 12 000 – is situated well within the Arctic Circle and relies heavily on fishing and hunting to sustain its fragile economy during the harsh winter months when visibility is poor.

b. Fishing and hunting are important to Uummannaq's economy in the winter.

c. Uummannaq relies heavily on the inhabitants' ability to catch fish such as halibut, cod and sea catfish especially in the hazardous winter months.

7. Which of these words and phrases are useful connectives to use in summary writing? Circle your answers.

and	whatever	however	yet	as opposed to
when	incidentally	very good	in comparison	because

8. When writing a summary why is it important to consider the audience before beginning your response?

----

9. Rewrite this short passage using a more appropriate register for a summary.

You wouldn't believe how small some of these Arctic towns are! They're like smaller than our estate and so boring to live in. I mean who would want to live in a place like that, where all they do is fish?

----

10. Now it is time to make an evaluation of your progress through this chapter. Circle your response.

a. How confident are you when:

● *Using collective nouns?*	very	quite	sometimes	not very	I need help
● *Recognising active and passive?*	very	quite	sometimes	not very	I need help
● *Using comparative suffixes?*	very	quite	sometimes	not very	I need help

b. Which statement best describes you? Tick your response.

a. *I know what a summary is but I'm not sure how to write one.* winter.

b. *I recognise the key elements of a summary and can write one but it's hard.*

c. *I'm confident that any summary I write will be succinct, accurate and appropriate.*

c. Write a question of your own about one key element of writing a successful summary. Have an answer ready and try the question out on someone you know.

----

4 Animals and us

Imagine you are one of the rescuers searching with your dog in a disaster area. It is dangerous and difficult work. You have to trust the animal to keep you both safe. Which of these characteristics do you think is most valuable in your dog and why?

| Its ability to follow instructions | Its sense of smell | Its loyalty to you | Its bravery |

The characteristic I find most valuable is

----

because

Disaster dogs

When an earthquake happens and survivors are trapped under mountains of rubble, time is the most important factor. It is **imperative** that rescuers work quickly and focus their efforts in the correct places. Here is where Search and Rescue (SAR) dogs are **invaluable**. These specially trained canines work closely with their handlers to sniff out any signs of human life using their **pronounced** sense of smell. Capable of covering large areas of **debris** very quickly, the work these dogs undertake allows rescuers to concentrate on specific locations where survivors may be found. This makes the whole rescue process quicker and more effective.

Research is still being conducted on how these disaster dogs operate, but it is thought that they are able to detect living humans through their scent. Humans lose skin cells at the rate of thousands every minute and it has been **proposed** that the unique scent attached to these cells is detected by the dogs. It may also be that the dogs can sense the **perspiration** given off by humans under stress. Although scientists are uncertain as to how the dogs do what they do, there is no doubting how successful they are in saving many lives in disaster areas.

A search and rescue team hunt for survivors

Building your vocabulary

imperative: essential or urgent

invaluable: having a value too great to be measured

pronounced: very noticeable or standing out

debris: scattered broken pieces and remains

proposed: suggested

perspiration: sweat

1. Without looking back at the text, what is SAR short for?

    ----

2. Circle the two reasons why dogs are used in disaster areas.

    a. They have a pronounced sense of smell and can detect human scent and perspiration.

    b. They are loyal to their owners.

    c. When sniffing for survivors they can cover large areas of ground very quickly.

    d. They don't need to eat or drink much when working.

3. If you were operating in a disaster area why might you find dogs an invaluable asset?

    ----

4. As a member of a search and rescue team, why is it so imperative that you work quickly among the debris?

    ----

5. Why do you think it is that scientists have proposed theories, but are still uncertain how these disaster dogs work so effectively?

    ----

6. If you were leading the search and rescue operation what advice would you give to your teams?

Similes and metaphors

Looking closely

Sometimes when writing, it is not enough to just describe a situation or explain an idea. It may be that the importance of the idea needs to be emphasised. One way of doing this is through the use of imagery. Similes and metaphors create appropriate images in the reader's mind.

Similes work by suggesting a comparison between two subjects using *like* or *as* to create the image.

- The search and rescue dog was as brave as a warrior.

When you think of a warrior you picture someone who is full of courage. By linking the rescue dog to a warrior because of its bravery the reader understands how courageous the dog is.

A metaphor is a more direct comparison than a simile.

- When an earthquake happens and survivors are trapped under *mountains of rubble*, time is the most important factor.

Here the writer is trying to make the reader understand how much rubble is left after an earthquake. Directly comparing it to *mountains* suggests the huge amount there is.

1. Using the words from the box complete these similes about the rescue dog.

   a gymnast   a laser beam   an arrow   a baby

   a. The rescue dog was as focused *as* ------------------.

   b. The rescue dog was *like* ------------------ as it pointed to where the survivor was buried in the debris.

   c. Once its mission was complete the rescue dog slept *like* ------------------.

   d. Without hesitation and as agile *as* ------------------, the rescue dog climbed over the rubble of the fallen building.

2. Create some similes about the rescue dog's mission. Compare the subjects in Box A with the ideas in Box B and try to be as imaginative as you can. The first one is done for you.

Box A	Box B
• The noise of the earthquake	• Thunder
• The tumbling of the buildings	• A waterfall
• The silence after the event	• Space
• The search for survivors	• A fearless hunter
• The dust that rose from the debris	• A sandstorm

   a. The noise of the earthquake was *as deafening as the loudest clap of thunder* you have ever heard.

   b. --

   c. --

   d. --

   e. --

3. a. Here are some animals with characteristics that might be useful to human rescuers in a search and rescue situation. Draw lines to match the animal to the characteristic. One is done for you.

Animal

Characteristic

a. mountain goat	i. an excellent climber
b. badger	ii. good at pulling heavy loads but stubborn
c. bear	iii. excellent hearing
d. bat	iv. good at digging
e. mongoose	v. strong and relentless
f. oxen	vi. quick and agile

b. Now create a metaphor for each match above to show how the comparison works. One is done for you.

a. They called him 'The Goat' within the team because no one else could climb as well as he could.

b. _____

_____

c. _____

_____

d. _____

_____

e. _____

_____

f. _____

_____

Teacher tip

One way of remembering the difference between a simile and metaphor is to think of a simile as being *similar to*, *like* or *as* something else. Then it follows that the metaphor is the other one.

The future tense

Looking closely

The future tense is used when writing about events that have yet to happen.

The use of *shall* or *will* between the subject and the verb is how the future tense is formed. For example:

- We *shall* fly together to the disaster zone.

In this example, the sentence has been written in the first person.

If the sentence is written in the second or third person *will* is used instead of *shall* when creating the future tense. For example:

- *You will* join the search and rescue team.
- *They will* find survivors using the rescue dogs.

To add emphasis *will* is used instead of *shall* for the first person, such as:

- We *will* fly together to the disaster zone.

To add emphasis *shall* is used instead of *will* in the second or third person.

1. Tick which of these sentences are written in the future tense.

   a. I shall always love animals.

   b. I am looking forward to seeing marine wildlife from the boat.

   c. We will always treat animals that are hurt.

   d. I will never forget the first elephant I saw in the wild.

   e. I am always ready to watch animal documentaries on television.

2. Rewrite these sentences by adding emphasis. Notice the difference it makes in each case.

   a. I shall enjoy going to the animal park tomorrow.

   ----

   b. Whenever it snows we shall watch the penguins skating on the ice.

   ----

   c. I shall laugh when I see the baby giraffe trying to walk when we visit the zoo.

   ----

3. The sentences below are written in the second and third person. Rewrite each sentence adding *will* to change it into the future tense.

   a. You love the movie about bears in Canada.

   ----

   b. He travels to see the big cats in the wild at last.

   ----

   c. She appreciates the chance to take some photographs on the safari.

   ----

   d. They understand how important it is to protect endangered species.

Looking closely

Depending on which tense is being used, the verb ending is different. Here is an example:

- Past: Max the Alsatian *spent* four years working in disaster areas.
- Present: Max the Alsatian *is spending* four years working in disaster areas.
- Future: Max the Alsatian *will spend* four years working in disaster areas.

4. Underline the correct verb ending to change these sentences into the future tense.

   a. Max will (*searched/searching/search*) for survivors to the best of his ability.

   b. Max will (*stop/stopped/stopping*) only when his handler commands him to.

   c. Max will (*barked/bark/barking*) when he finds a survivor and will (*stood/standing/stand*) by the place until his handler arrives.

5. Convert this paragraph into the future tense.

   > Yesterday I watched a really fascinating programme about how search and rescue dogs were trained. I never took them for granted and I remembered how unselfish they were. When they went to disaster areas I worried whether they would survive the terrible conditions.

Teacher tip

It is important to be able to recognise and write in the past, present or future tense to improve your understanding and performance. Practise changing short texts such as news articles into a different tense.

Adverbs

Looking closely

An adverb gives additional information about a verb, adjective or even another adverb. This process is called modifying. For example:

- The trained rescue dog *boldly* searched for the missing child.

In this sentence *searched* is the verb that is modified by the adverb *boldly*. The reader knows that the dog not only searched for the child, but did so with confidence. Here are some more examples of how adverbs can modify verbs:

- Both trainer and dog *safely* climbed the steep ramp to the rescue ship.
- Rescues are often hampered by *poorly* acquired intelligence of an area.
- Rescue dogs are *warmly* welcomed by those they save.

1. The box contains 16 adverbs. Use nine of these to fill the missing gaps in the passage.

completely	slowly	occasionally	gracefully	usually	sometimes
eagerly	often	always	normally	successfully	rudely
loosely	anxiously	regularly	unexpectedly		

Max is a 5-year-old male Alsatian who ------------------ works with his handler on rescue missions in mountainous regions. When off duty, Max ------------------ waits for the chance to show off his skills. He ------------------ trains for up to four hours a day, but ------------------ for longer, so that he is ------------------ ready for action. He is ------------------ loyal to his handler. When in action Max has been trained to climb ------------------ over rocky terrain, but when the conditions are really bad even he ------------------ encounters difficulties in ------------------ tracking lost mountaineers.

2. Now it is your turn. Use five of the ten adverbs in the box to create your own sentences. Try to maintain the theme of animals.

technically	badly	nervously	obediently	promptly
frequently	never	deliberately	accidentally	lazily

a. --

b. --

c. --

d. --

e. --

Looking closely

Sometimes an adverb is replaced in a sentence by an adverbial phrase. An adverbial phrase is two or more words used together in place of an adverb to modify the verb. For example:

- When training a rescue dog, it is better to wait *for a second* before repeating the order.

In this sentence the verb *wait* is modified by the adverbial phrase *for a second*. This is an example of an adverbial phrase used to indicate time. Adverbial phrases can also be used to indicate place and manner.

3. Place these nine adverbial phrases in the correct box.

in a while	across the road	in an angry tone
after some time	without slowing down	for a moment
in silence	into empty space	along the walkway

Time – when it happens

Place – where it happens

Manner – how it happens

4. Now it is time to practise your use of adverbial phrases. Use three of the nine phrases in your own sentences. Here is an example:

- *In a while* the rescue dog will start to search for the scent again.

a. _____

b. _____

c. _____

5. Write a sentence using your own adverbial phrase.

_____

_____

Teacher tip

Many adverbs end in *–ly* but, like some examples already given, this is not always the case. Research and learn some more common adverbs that do not follow this rule.

Writing in response to points of view

Keeping animals in zoos remains an issue that divides opinion. What do you think?

- Zoos save animals that will become extinct.

- Zoos cage animals that should be free.

- Zoos are a necessary evil because caging animals is wrong, but some need to be protected.

I think zoos are _____

because _____

Guidance

How you present a written argument will determine whether the reader is convinced or not. Rhetorical questions and the rule of three are some of the techniques you can use.

Rhetorical questions are ones that are asked for effect, without expecting an answer. They can be powerful in persuading a reader to agree with your point of view. Here is an example:

- Surely you must agree that zoos are places that protect animals?

The question contains the answer. By stating *surely you must agree* the writer aims to convince the reader to agree by giving the impression that any other viewpoint would be wrong.

By placing three examples together to prove your point you can add weight to your argument. This is known as the rule of three and emphasises that your point is a good one. Here is an example:

- Zoos are costly to run, never have big enough paddocks and rarely employ fully trained staff.

Here, three arguments why zoos are bad are placed together to create a convincing point.

1. Tick which of these are rhetorical questions.

    a. Do you believe zoos are outdated in the 21st century?

    b. Will you consider that zoos are the answer to species going extinct?

    c. Surely, zoos do serve an important purpose in preserving species, don't they?

    d. You must agree without doubt that if there were no zoos many animal groups would be extinct by now?

    e. Haven't I said it enough times that supporting zoos is the wrong thing to do?

2. Write a sentence including an example of the rule of three for each viewpoint.

    a. Animals are happy in zoos.

    _____

    b. Animals don't belong in zoos.

    _____

3. Think about the argument that zoos allow you to view animals you might not otherwise be able to see. Read the passage below and then answer the questions about the language used.

> I had seen hundreds of images of elephants online but nothing prepared me for the magical experience of viewing one of these magnificent beasts in the flesh for the first time. No image could ever portray the enormous size, raw power and overwhelming presence of an adult male standing just a few metres away. Nor could a mere image successfully convey the sensory experience; the musky smell of the habitat, the trumpeting sound of its call or the sheer grace of its movement. Truly being up close and personal is a memory that will last for a lifetime. Who says zoos are bad?

a. Which sentence is an example of a rhetorical question?

----

b. The rule of three is used twice in the passage. Underline each example.

c. What is the overall effect on the reader of using the words *magical, magnificent* and *enormous* in the passage?

----

d. Which other words used add to this effect?

Changing the emphasis

4. The passage written by the writer who thinks it is a good idea to see an elephant in a zoo offers one viewpoint. By creating an alternative viewpoint, elephants' welfare is now most important. Read the passage and then answer the questions below.

> In this modern world where technology allows us to experience these great creatures from the comfort of our own homes, surely there is no justification for keeping them penned in what to an elephant must seem a confined, limited and depressingly small place? Will any sane elephant choose to live in an area where it cannot roam free? We are lying to ourselves if we imagine we are doing these great and noble creatures a favour by locking them in paddocks, forcing them to breed at our will and constantly watching their every move. They deserve to be free.

a. Again, the rule of three is used twice. Underline the two examples.

b. Which sentence is an example of a rhetorical question?

----

c. How effective is the concluding sentence in putting over the viewpoint of the passage?

Are zoos still necessary in the 21st century?

Planning

You are going to write a balanced essay of about 200 words on the issue of zoos.

Here are some arguments for and against zoos. You will need to discuss both sides of the argument and consider both viewpoints.

For zoos

- They protect endangered species
- They run breeding programmes to make sure species survive
- They offer a chance for people to see animals normally they wouldn't see
- Animals are more safe in a zoo than in the wild

Against zoos

- Animals are caged not free
- The animals are on show for the benefit of people and not for their own protection
- Animals are taken from the wild to live in zoos
- Animals do not behave normally in zoos because their instincts change

1. You may want to carry out some more research, but here are some facts and statistics to help you. Decide whether each is **for** or **against** zoos. Put a capital **F** or **A** in each box.

	F or A
Zoos work together to breed endangered species.	
In UK zoos, 75 per cent of elephants are overweight.	
A Species Survival Plan in zoos is preserving the black lemur from extinction.	
Tigers in zoos have 1/18 000th of the room to roam that they have in the wild.	
African elephants live three times longer in the wild.	
Worldwide over 700 million people visit zoos each year.	
Some zoos train animals to perform tricks to attract visitors.	
Only 45 Amur leopards survive in the wild, but there are 220 in zoos.	

2. An effective introductory sentence is very important. Tick which of these you think is the most effective.

   a. I like zoos because they are fun to visit and I don't understand people who hate them.

   b. In the 21st century zoos have come under increasing pressure from those who argue they are no longer needed, but statistics show that every year 700 million people visit zoos across the world.

   c. Zoos are bad for the animals and only there to provide entertainment for people who don't care that the animals are suffering.

Now write your own introductory sentence.

----

3. Your conclusion should not be too long but it is important you end strongly.

   a. Why is the following conclusion poor?

      It is up to you to decide whether zoos are good or bad as I am not sure what I think.

      I think this is poor because _____

      _____

      _____

   b. Write your own stronger and better conclusion here. Remember it is important to know where you are going to end before you begin your plan.

      _____

      _____

4. The next step is to make a plan so your response is organised appropriately. Write your plan in the box below. One of your points is done for you as a guide.

My plan:

Introduction	– Refer to the task title and introduce both sides of the argument.
First point	– Animals are not free, but endangered species are protected.
Second point	– _____
Third point	– _____
Fourth point	– _____
Conclusion	– _____

Writing

5. Now on a separate sheet of paper write your 200-word balanced essay about the following question:

- Are zoos still necessary in the 21st century?

Skills checklist

When you have finished your balanced essay, complete the following checklist.

? Have you identified all four points in your plan?

? Have you covered both sides of the argument for each point?

? Have you started with a strong introductory sentence and ended with a strong concluding comment?

? Have you considered using rhetorical questions and the rule of three?

? Have you considered making every word count?

? Have you been clear on what your own, considered view is?

Checking your progress

1. Mahatma Ghandi once said: "The greatness of a nation and its moral progress can be judged by the way its animals are treated." Write a quote that sums up how you feel about animals.

Grammar

2. Read this sentence and then answer the two questions.

    ● When necessary, any mother is like a lioness defending her cubs.

    a. Which word tells you this is a simile? _____.

    b. Use the idea of a mother being like a lioness to make a metaphor.

    ----

3. Match these words and phrases to create two suitable similes. Be as creative as you can.

    > graceful   wise   ballet dancer   swan   headteacher   owl

    a. --

    b. --

4. Change this passage into the future tense.

    > Last week I walked to school on two days. Each day I saw the same snake fast asleep in the middle of the path. It was a viper so I crossed the road and quickly ran to avoid disturbing it. By the time I reached school I was very frightened and kept looking over my shoulder to make sure the snake was not following.

    ----

5. Underline the adverbs or adverbial phrases in these sentences.

    a. After a while the crocodile swam gracefully away from the boat.

    b. Purposefully creeping, soundlessly breathing and watching intensely, the lioness approached the herd.

Writing

6. Put these statements in order, with the most balanced being number 1 and the least being 3.

    a. Lions are lazy and tigers aren't.

    b. Both lions and tigers are apex predators that conserve their energy by sleeping when they aren't hunting and both make fascinating viewing for lovers of big cats.

    c. Lions sleep a lot and so do tigers, but they are still interesting to watch.

7. Which of these is not an example of the rule of three? Tick your answer.

   a. I love animals because they are wild and exciting and I want to be a zoo keeper.

   b. I love the atmosphere in a zoo; the variety of smells, the different sounds and the way each animal has a character of its own.

8. Both of the following statements use the same basic fact, but they give out very different messages.

   a. Many zoos worldwide cooperate in breeding species thought to be in danger of extinction.

     Which key words or phrases suggest a positive message?

     ----

   b. Zoos across the world conspire to breed only those species that guarantee visitors through their gates.

     Which key words or phrases suggest a negative message?

     ----

9. Rewrite this passage to change the emphasis to supporting zoos.

> Nothing about zoos amazes or excites me. They're just prisons where innocent animals are caged and left to live in misery for their whole lives. I hate walking around these places, watching animals that should be free being forced to perform circus tricks and restlessly pace around their fenced enclosures. So what if some species become extinct in the wild? At least they've lived full and free lives!

----

10. Now it is time to make an evaluation of your progress through this chapter. Circle your response.

   a. How confident are you when:

• *Creating similes and metaphors?*	very	quite	sometimes	not very	I need help
• *Writing in the present tense?*	very	quite	sometimes	not very	I need help
• *Using adverbs and adverbial phrases?*	very	quite	sometimes	not very	I need help

   b. Which statement best describes you? Tick your response.

     a. *I know writing can have different points of view, but they are hard to find.*

     b. *I recognise different viewpoints, but it is hard for me to explain them in my own words.*

     c. *I'm confident that I understand balance and can explain viewpoints accurately and appropriately.*

   c. Now write a question of your own about how to write a balanced argument. Have an answer ready and try it out on someone you know.

     ----

5 Working life

If you were choosing a career to begin when leaving education what quality would be most important to you?

> **Being interesting**   **Working with great people**   **Being close to home**

The quality I would find most important is

----

because

Be prepared

Being in full-time education may seem hard at times, but it seems easy compared with the **traumatic** nature of deciding what to do when you leave. Choosing a career can be filled with difficult decisions and **numerous** questions. "What am I really good at? Will I be happy? Where will this career take me?" The more you sit and **contemplate,** the more questions you will think of and the fewer answers you will find.

So, how do you begin to **navigate** a way through what may well be the most important decision you have made in your life so far? There is an old saying that "being forewarned is being forearmed". Simply put, this means that the more prepared you are, the more likely you are to have the knowledge and understanding to make the correct decision. It is good advice. Today, more than any time in the past, you have the **opportunity** to seek what is available, find out all you need to know about the career you are thinking about and be prepared before you have to choose. Such is the power of the Internet. Choosing your first job need not be scary or **perplexing** if you take the time to prepare well and complete your research before you make your choice.

Building your vocabulary

traumatic: unpleasant and upsetting

numerous: many

contemplate: think about

navigate: steer or find a way through

opportunity: chance

perplexing: puzzling, confusing

1. What is full-time education?

    ----

2. Underline the three reasons why choosing a career can be difficult according to the writer.

    a. There are so many questions to contemplate about which career will be best.

    b. Choices can be perplexing and difficult to navigate.

    c. Some careers pay better wages than others.

    d. Not all the numerous questions you think of will have answers.

3. Why does the writer think leaving education to begin a career is so traumatic?

    ----

4. How necessary is it for a young person choosing a career to be "forewarned and forearmed"?

    ----

5. How are students today given more opportunity to make the correct decision when choosing a career?

    ----

6. If you were helping a friend to choose a new career what advice would you give?

Borrowed words

Looking closely

English continues to lend words to other languages, but also borrows words. The English language includes many words that have been borrowed from places around the world. Words like these started out being used by a few individuals, but over time have become known by lots of people and used in everyday conversations.

Although science and technology largely borrows words from Latin, the biggest number of borrowed words in everyday English use comes from French. The close distance and shared history has lead to all kinds of French words entering the English language. Here are some examples:

- *garage*   a building where cars are kept or a place where petrol is sold

- *shock*   an unpleasant surprise.

Anyone who wears *denim jeans* should know that both words are borrowed from the French language.

1. Latin is an ancient language from which many English words have been borrowed. Complete the sentences using borrowed words from the list below.

   > butter   pepper   wine   kettle   kitchen

   a. _____ is made from cream and can be spread on bread.

   b. You can boil water in a _____.

   c. If you want to be a successful chef you need to know your way around a _____.

   d. _____ is often served with a meal in restaurants in England.

2. In any job that involves travel you will use some borrowed Latin words. Read the passage below and then find the Latin word to go with its meaning. The first one is done for you.

   > I had to drive to a city last week on business. As I approached it, I drove along the street next to the city walls and past an old town hall. I became lost and ended up going around in circles for several miles trying to find the office where my meeting was taking place.

   a. These are round and have no sides.   _____ circles _____

   b. Units of distance used in the UK today.   _____

   c. A place where many people live that is bigger than a town.   _____

   d. Buildings usually have four of these, one on each side.   _____

   e. Cars drive down this and houses are built by it.   _____

   f. The main administrative building in a town.   _____

Looking closely

When the Scandinavians invaded Britain and settled there they also took their language with them. These include some very common words such as *give* and *take*.

3. Write a sentence for each of the borrowed words below showing their correct meaning.

   a. hit: _____

   b. leg: _____

   c. sky: _____

   d. they: _____

4. English borrows words from nearly every culture it has been in contact with. Here is a fun exercise to see how good your knowledge of world languages is. Match the borrowed words to the language they originally came from. The first one is done for you.

African languages	Arabic	Australian English	Hindi
Italian	Japanese	American Indian languages	Spanish

   a. zebra — gorilla — banana — = _African languages_

   b. kangaroo — boomerang — koala — = _____

   c. bazaar — mosque — caravan — = _____

   d. bungalow — jungle — shampoo — = _____

   e. sushi — judo — tsunami — = _____

   f. guitar — tornado — mosquito — = _____

   g. piano — pizza — umbrella — = _____

   h. chocolate — tomato — canoe — = _____

5. Complete the paragraph using borrowed words from the box.

excellent	tour	they	journey	explored	dragon
pay	theatre	café	science	dance	perform

Earlier this year I went on holiday to Paris. My _____ took three hours. On my first morning I had breakfast in a _____ then I took a _____ of the city. In the afternoon I _____ the West Bank on my own. In the evening I went to a _____ to watch a _____ show. It was about a hero fighting a terrible fire-breathing _____ As a _____ teacher I do not really believe in such animals but I was happy to _____ for a ticket to watch the dancers _____ such a good show. _____ were all _____

Jargon

Looking closely

Jargon refers to words and phrases used by specific groups of people that may not be understood by those outside the groups. Professionals such as those in medicine and law use a set of words and phrases that have meaning to them within their workplace, but not to others.

One of the areas where a lot of jargon is used is the world of computing. Words and phrases have been created to describe new ideas in this area. Here are some examples:

> byte   gigabyte   terabyte

A *byte* is used to measure storage space on a computer or disk. There are about 1000 *bytes* in a *gigabyte* and about 1000 *gigabytes* in a *terabyte*.

1. Complete these sentences using computer jargon from the list below.

> software   processor   malware   database   spam

    a. The part of the computer that acts like a brain is called a _____.

    b. A program that organises information on a computer and lets you search is called a _____.

    c. A computer program that creates documents is an example of _____.

    d. A software program that is made to cause harm to your computer is called _____.

    e. Unwanted email junk is sometimes called _____.

Looking closely

Words and phrases often become abbreviated by those who use them often. These shortened versions are also jargon. For example:

- Artificial Intelligence is referred to as *AI*.

2. Draw lines to match the abbreviation to the long version. One is done for you.

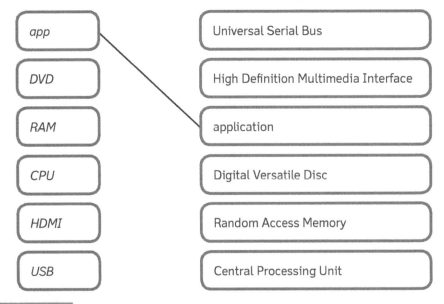

app	Universal Serial Bus
DVD	High Definition Multimedia Interface
RAM	application
CPU	Digital Versatile Disc
HDMI	Random Access Memory
USB	Central Processing Unit

Looking closely

Jargon can be new words or words that have been reused to give new meaning in a specific field. There are many examples in computing, such as:

- port   a place on a computer where other devices can be added
- bit   the smallest unit of information in a computer program
- memory   the part of the computer that remembers the information.

There is a connection to the original meaning, for example: a port is a place where a ship docks to load or unload its cargo, so the action of joining to add or take away is the same.

Sometimes the same word is used, but the spelling is altered to show the specific meaning, for instance:

- computer *program*   as opposed to television *programme*.

3. All five words below have been reused in computing to have a different specific meaning. Read the original meanings and add your explanation of the new meaning to show the difference. The first one is done for you.

> attachment   mouse   burn   crash   bug

a. An <u>attachment</u> only used to be a noun meaning friendship or an extra part added to a piece of equipment, but now it is also *a file added to an email*.

b. A <u>mouse</u> only used to be a little furry mammal, but now it is also

----

----

c. The verb to <u>burn</u> only used to mean to damage something by fire or heat, but now it also means

----

----

d. The verb to <u>crash</u> only used to mean to have a violent accident or to fail suddenly, but now it also means

----

----

e. The word <u>bug</u> had several meanings already: an insect; a micro-organism; a secret microphone; a virus or a passion for something, but now also means

----

Teacher tip

Jargon is useful when discussing a specific field, such as computing, medicine or law. Jargon is also used a lot in sports such as football, cricket and athletics.

Possessives

Remember

Possessives are words that show connections. They make clear to whom or what something belongs. Possessive adjectives work in a similar way to other adjectives by adding more information to a noun. They show what belongs to someone or something. In a sentence the possessive adjective is placed before the noun it belongs to, so the relationship between the two is clear.

Looking closely

There are seven possessive adjectives to learn, as shown below.

Singular: *her*   *his*   *its*   *my*   *your*

Plural: *our*   *their*

Here are two sentences showing examples of their use:

- Sadly *her* bus was late so she missed *her* interview.

- *Their* interviews were on Thursday and they were all very nervous about *their* prospects.

1. Add a correct singular possessive adjective to each sentence below. For some sentences, more than one of the options could be correct.

   a. I asked my brother if _____ job is exciting.

   b. I wondered whether my sister drove _____ car to work this morning.

   c. "_____ chances of getting this job are very good," I told my friend.

   d. The new department store opened _____ doors for the first time today.

   e. I am not sure I will ever finish _____ job application.

   f. If _____ sister works late _____ friend gives her a lift home, but if _____

   brother works late he has to make _____ way home on foot.

2. Add the correct plural possessive adjective to complete the sentences below.

   a. When we travel to work each day _____ train is always late arriving.

   b. All the people on the train are frustrated and _____ faces look very angry.

   c. _____ boss is always annoyed by _____ lateness, but it isn't _____ fault if the train is late.

   d. _____ boss just tells us to look around the office at all the other workers at _____ desks

   on time and tells us that _____ timekeeping is not a problem.

Looking closely

The possessive pronouns are: *hers, his, its, mine, ours, theirs* and *yours*.

Pronouns replace nouns or noun phrases in a sentence. This avoids repeating the noun or noun phrase, which helps the flow of the writing. Possessive pronouns serve the same purpose, but they also show belonging in the same way possessive adjectives do. For instance:

- The manager welcomed back a former employee of the manager. *This becomes*:

- The manager welcomed back a former employee of <u>his</u>.

In this example the former employee belongs to the manager, so instead of making the sentence sound awkward by using *the manager* twice, *his* can be used instead.

3. Underline the correct possessive pronoun to complete each sentence. The first one is done for you.

   a. Why did you sit in that seat when you know it is (*yours*/<u>*mine*</u>/*ours*)?

   b. John has a great office. Of all the offices in the building (*hers/his/ours*) is the best.

   c. I like my job but (*yours/mine/its*) is better and you are paid more!

   d. Sarah took control in the meetings so (*his/yours/hers*) always finished on time.

   e. I'm glad we finished our project first. (*Ours/Mine/Its*) will definitely be chosen. The other group's project was late. (*Theirs/Hers/Ours*) was not as good as (*its/his/ours*).

4. Rewrite this passage replacing the nouns and noun phrases with possessive pronouns, where it is appropriate to do so.

   > I work in a hotel. The hotel's rooms are the best in the city. There are many places to stay, but all who work here agree none are better than our hotel. My wife and I both have jobs in the hotel. My wife's job is in reception and my job is in the restaurant. Other people we meet lead such very busy lives compared to our lives. Other people's busy lives are full of travelling and meetings, but my wife and my lives are happy. We work long hours because we love being at the hotel. The hotel's atmosphere is really friendly.

Planning and writing a job application

Writing about yourself can be very easy or very hard. What do you think?

- I dislike writing about myself because I never know what to say.

- I love writing about myself because I am so interesting.

- I prefer not to write about myself but I can do it when I need to.

Writing about myself is

----

because

Guidance

A job application is a formal piece of writing. It should be written in a suitable style that makes clear both your ability to write formal English and your own skills and strengths as a person. Unlike other formal pieces, this can be written in the first person because you are the subject.

When planning any piece of written work it is useful to make notes to help you. When making notes you should:

- use bullet points

- do not use full sentences – short and relevant works best

- concentrate on key ideas only

- include relevant and specific details rather than general points.

1. Read this advertisement for a job as an office junior in a law firm. Now look at the phrases in the box on page 69. Choose three phrases that you think are the key points given in the advertisement. Write each one against a bullet point below.

> Wanted: an office junior to join a very successful and busy law firm. Applicants should be educated to Grade C level or equivalent, have good written, verbal communication and computing skills. Applicants should be able to use text documents, spreadsheets and presentation software. Duties will include filing, answering telephone and email enquiries, collating documents and general office tasks. A flexible approach will be expected. In addition, applicants should be confident, show initiative when needed, but also be capable of following instructions and working to strict deadlines. The successful applicant will need to dress appropriately for a working office and behave professionally at all times. Office hours are 8am to 5pm Monday to Friday, with applicants also expected to work some weekends when necessary.

Academic success	A good range of skills	Professional qualities	Flexible approach to work
Work hard	Good at answering the telephone	Dress neatly	Timekeeper

- --
- --
- --

2. Take your first bullet point and make some notes below by writing the key details in the box. An example is given to help you.

- A good range of skills. Key details:

  ----

3. Now write your paragraph based on the first bullet point and the notes you have made. Try to write about 50 words.

----

4. Making notes is an important skill to learn. To practise, choose any text you are interested in, such as a newspaper or magazine article, webpage or even an instruction manual, and make notes in the same way as you have done on these two pages.

Your application for a job

Planning

You are going to plan and write a job application of about 150 words.

For a job application you must use a formal writing style. You are trying to impress your audience through the words you write and the way you write them. Remember these points when using a formal writing style:

- Write in the first person in an application, but do not address the reader directly.
- Do not use contractions and abbreviations.
- Avoid using informal phrases, idioms, slang or text language.
- Correct punctuation and grammar are very important.
- Begin paragraphs with topic sentences.

1. Which one of these introductions is most suitable for a formal application? Why?

   a. Dear Sir,

   I would like to apply for the post of trainee accountant as advertised in *The Times* on Monday 14th June.

   b. Hi,

   My name is John Smith and I'd like to put my name forward for the job you've advertised.

   c. Dear Sir,

   I'm very keen and eager to work for you and I won't give up until I do. I'm a great person and will be brilliant at the job advertised.

   Internet

   I think _____ is the most suitable because _____

   _____

Guidance

Topic sentences are the opening sentence in a paragraph and introduce the subject for that paragraph. Any other sentences in the paragraph should be connected to the same idea.

For example, a paragraph about your personal skills could begin:

- I possess a number of personal skills that make me suitable for this post.

The rest of the paragraph will then explain these skills.

2. Read the topic sentences below and then explain the subject each one introduces.

   a. I have achieved outstanding academic success in my studies.

   _____

   b. I have always been interested in meeting new people and serving the public.

   _____

3. Use the notes you took on pages 68–69 and your new knowledge of topic sentences to help you plan your application. Follow the steps and guidance below:

- Choose the job you are going to apply for.

- Base your introduction on the correct answer in question 1.

- Aim for three main paragraphs after your introduction.

Complete your plan below by writing your introduction and topic sentences for the other paragraphs.

Plan

Your chosen job title: _____

Introduction: _____

_____

_____

Paragraph 1: _____

_____

Paragraph 2: _____

_____

Paragraph 3: _____

_____

Writing

4. Now use your plans and on a separate sheet of paper write about 150 words to complete the following task:

- Write an application for a job of your choice.

Skills checklist

When you have finished your formal application, complete the following checklist.

? Have you used your notes to write three topic sentences?

? Have you completed a plan using these topic sentences?

? Have you developed your points based on the topic sentences?

? Have you written in a formal style?

? Have you made every word count?

Checking your progress

1. Confucius wrote: "Choose a job you love, and you will never have to work a day in your life." Write a quote that sums up how you feel about choosing a career.

Grammar

2. Read the text below and answer the following question. What are these all examples of?

> City – Latin   Ballet – French   Sky – Scandinavian   Canoe – American Indian

----

3. Underline the computer jargon used in the following sentence.

   I use the Internet every day to look at interesting webpages, read blogs and receive emails though I really hate all the spam and am scared of hackers.

4. Underline the correct possessive adjectives in this passage.

   (*My/His/Her*) brother and I have always wanted to work with cars. (*Its/His/Her*) dream is to own a Ferrari. (*Its/Our/Their*) appearance and power fascinate him. (*Her/Their/Our*) sister thinks we are mad. Together with (*its/her/their*) friend she dreams of being a movie star. All (*their/her/our*) spare time is spent watching old movies, so they know how to act and walk. Now who's crazy?

5. Underline the possessive pronouns in each sentence below.

   a. Her dream job is okay, but ours is great. Hers will never happen.

   b. Some mechanics I know claim theirs is the best job ever, but I believe mine is better.

   c. I must admit Sam is lucky to work as a reporter for *The Times*. Its stories are always the most accurate but mine are mostly made up.

   d. I don't want to do what my brother does so can I choose the same career as you? Yours looks so interesting but his is boring.

Writing

6. When making notes which of these statements apply? Tick your answers.

   a. Use full sentences

   b. Keep your notes short but relevant

   c. Make general comments

   d. Concentrate on key ideas only

7. Make three notes on the following subject: My ideal career.

 a. --

 b. --

 c. --

8. Which one is the topic sentence in this paragraph? Underline your answer.

> I possess excellent written and verbal communication skills. I have written articles for the school magazine and one of these was published in the local newspaper too. I am a member of the school debating team that took part in a national competition and was placed second overall. I have presented to the governors on a number of occasions in my role as a member of the school council.

9. Rewrite this passage using a formal style.

> Hi, I'd like to apply to be a nurse. I've always wanted to be one as it'd be my dream job. I'm confident I'm good enough and would give it a good go. I'm a people person so no worries there. Please give me a ring if I get an interview.

----

10. Now it is time to make an evaluation of your progress through this chapter. Circle your response.

 a. How confident are you when:

• *Using jargon?*	very	quite	sometimes	not very	I need help
• *Using possessive adjectives?*	very	quite	sometimes	not very	I need help
• *Using possessive pronouns?*	very	quite	sometimes	not very	I need help

 b. Which statement best describes you? Tick your response.

 a. *I know what note making is, but find it hard to find the key ideas.*

 b. *I recognise key ideas, but it is hard for me to make short relevant notes.*

 c. *I'm confident that I understand how to make notes that will be useful when writing my response to a task.*

 c. Write a question of your own about how to make notes. Have an answer ready and try it out on someone you know.

In a desert you will certainly find sand, but can you think of other things you can see there too? Write down a few. Try to think of six.

a. -- b. --

c. -- d. --

e. -- f. --

The Rub'al Khali Desert is the largest non-stop sand desert in the world, crossing Saudi Arabia, Oman, Yemen and the United Arab Emirates (UAE). It is also known as the Empty Quarter. Two people who attempted to cross it are Alastair Humphreys and Leon McCarron, in the footsteps of explorer Wilfred Thesiger.

Wilfred Thesiger made a **series** of journeys on the Arabian Peninsula in the 1940's. …

The Empty Quarter, or *Rub' al Khali*, is the largest sand desert on Earth. It **sprawls** across Oman, the United Arab Emirates, Yemen and Saudi Arabia. …

I considered doing the trip by myself. But I wanted to produce a beautiful film of the story and that is something better done by two people. There would be no **support vehicles**, back-up crew or cameramen. …

I emailed Leon McCarron … despite not knowing him very well at all. …

He was a fellow fan of Thesiger and liked the idea of making another film. …

We quickly began planning. We could not afford camels, had no idea how to drive one, and found them quite scary anyway. So instead we would be human camels, **hauling** a homemade cart filled with cheap supplies for 1000 miles across the Empty Quarter. We would begin in Salalah, as

Thesiger had done. We would finish in Dubai. Why Dubai? We chose Dubai because it would **illustrate** nicely how Arabia has changed since Thesiger's time. …

We designed the cart ourselves … We bought wheels online. … We didn't have time to test these before we flew to Oman. Needless to say these turned out to be the wrong size too!

Source: http://www.alastairhumphreys.com/a-bit-of-background-to-into-the-empty-quarter/

Building your vocabulary

series: several of the same type

sprawls: spreads out in an irregular way

support vehicle: car or truck with provisions and medical aid

hauling: pulling along with difficulty

illustrate: to show, or to serve as an example of

1. Who inspired Alistair to make the journey across the Empty Quarter?

   ----

2. Why did Alistair ask Leon to go with him?

   ----

3. Why does Alistair say he and Leon were wrong to design their cart themselves?

   ----

4. Give two reasons why you think their journey would not have been easy.

   ----

5. Why do people find challenges like this a positive thing to do?

   ----

6. Explain why you would or would not have liked to join Alistair on his journey.

The past continuous

Looking closely

There are two parts to the past continuous. You create it with *was/were* (the past of *to be*) and the *–ing* form of the main verb you are using. You use the past continuous to describe an action started in the past that is still going on.

We also use the past continuous to describe an action in the past that was interrupted by another action. For example:

- Jack *was running* down the road when he <u>saw</u> Pete.
- The bus *was moving* quite fast when it <u>crashed</u> into a bush.

1. Place the given verb into the past continuous in the following sentences.

   a. Moby ----------------------- his new bike to work. (ride)

   b. I --------------------- a letter to Bob this morning. (write)

   c. Hee Mok ---------------------- on a train going to his new job. (sitting)

   d. Juan and Pablo ---------------------- their suitcases to go on holiday. (pack)

   e. Jake and Mary ---------------------- for the first time. (fly)

Teacher tip

Use the past continuous main verb to help give some background to another past event as it will make your writing more interesting.

2. Add a suitable past continuous verb to complete the sentences below.

   a. I --------------------- my car when my phone rang.

   b. He --------------------- dinner when he heard a crash.

   c. They --------------------- to catch the bus when one of them fell over.

   d. We --------------------- to go to Australia, but unfortunately I broke my leg.

   e. She --------------------- to start her car when her neighbour came over to help her.

Looking closely

Let's have a look at the differences in meaning that different verb tenses can create. Here are two sentences:

- I *was walking* along the road when my phone rang.
- I *had walked* down the road when my phone rang.

In the first example you are still walking, and the continuous tense tells us this. Your phone rang while you were walking.

In the second example your phone still rings, but it is after you have walked down the road.

Did you spot the verb tense in the second example? Yes, it is the past perfect tense.

3. Underline the past continuous verbs in the diary entry below.

> Last week we were walking through the forest. We were trying to go very quietly because we didn't want to frighten any of the animals. Everything was going well when suddenly…

4. Complete these sentences using the past continuous or the past perfect form of the verb in brackets.

For example:

- Jake was talking to his friend when he saw a taxi stop outside his house. (talk)

a. Amy ---------------------- tennis with her friends when her telephone rang. (play)

b. The pedestrian light ---------------------- green when Mo crossed the road. (turn)

c. Ivy ---------------------- her garden when it started to rain. (water)

d. Costas ---------------------- every evening to prepare for the exam at the weekend. (study)

e. Esther baked a new cake because her children ---------------------- the first one she made. (eat)

5. Now continue the diary entry in exercise 3 and use the past continuous at least twice. Aim to write another 40 words.

----

6. Write five sentences using the past continuous about a recent exciting journey you made. For example:

- This morning, I was waiting at the coach stop with my friends.

a. ---

b. ---

c. ---

d. ---

e. ---

Relative pronouns

> ## Remember
>
> A relative pronoun connects a clause to a noun or pronoun to describe one thing. These are examples:
>
> - *Who* and *whose* are used to describe people and their possessions.
> - *Where* is used to describe a place.
> - After a noun, *that* gives a description needed to work out what the noun refers to. For example:
>
>   She picked up the kitten *that* was asleep
>
>   means there was more than one kitten, only one was asleep, and she picked up that one.
> - *Which* also gives a description, but it is not needed to work out what the noun refers to. For example:
>
>   She picked up the kitten *which* was asleep
>
>   means that there was only one kitten, that it was asleep, and she picked it up.

1. Underline the relative pronoun in each sentence and the noun or pronoun it is referring to. For example:
    - India is a place where many people live.
    a. The bicycle that is over there is mine.
    b. The green fields where I live are very beautiful.
    c. I like Australia because it is where I learned how to scuba dive.
    d. My geography teacher is someone who has travelled to nearly every country in the world.

2. Draw lines to match the start of the sentences on the left with the endings on the right. Look at the relative pronouns to help you choose the right ending.

a. Mike is my teacher	i. where I have always wanted to go.
b. Brazil is a country	ii. who taught me all about map-reading.
c. Keith is a guitar player	iii. that is played all over the world.
d. K-pop is a type of music	iv. whose band is world-famous.

3. Now add a relative pronoun to the following sentences. For example:
    - The boy who came first was given a gold medal.
    a. The trainers over there, _____ owners have left them behind, will be thrown away if they are not claimed by Friday.
    b. The shop keeper, _____ was an athlete when he was younger, can hardly walk these days.
    c. My mother asked me last night _____ my blue coat was.
    d. I told my teacher _____ I had done all my homework.

Antecedents

Looking closely

An antecedent is an earlier word, phrase, or clause to which another word (especially a following relative pronoun) refers back. For example:

- I saw *Jacob* and gave *him* a map.

(*Him* refers back to Jacob in this sentence.)

The antecedent and the pronoun must always agree – a singular antecedent needs a singular pronoun, and a plural antecedent needs a plural noun. For example:

- The *coaches* are here and *they* are ready to leave.

Also, the gender must agree. For example:

- *Maria* came to the house and *she* was very happy.

4. Rewrite these sentences so the antecedent and the pronoun agree and are clear.

   a. I love my uncle so I bought her a present.

   ----

   b. Max ran away from Stefan so he kept running.

   ----

   c. The train left too soon. He was late. It missed him.

   ----

5. Now create a sentence of your own that confuses the pronoun and antecedent. Have some fun with it!

Teacher tip

Avoid having two nouns of the same gender and only one pronoun. For example:

- Peter and Alexander were talking about sport and <u>he</u> said he likes football.

In this sentence it is not clear who *he* refers to. Try this instead:

- When he was talking to Alexander, Peter said *he* likes football.

Modal verbs

Looking closely

Modals verbs talk about possible and probable outcomes and also show what is needed for an outcome to occur. Here are the verbs we call modal verbs:

can	could	may	might
must	will	would	

Modal verbs are used with another main verb and show the likelihood of the main verb.

You use modal verbs to show how likely something is to happen or what is needed for something to happen. For example:

- We may go canoeing next week. (quite likely)
- We might go to Brazil on holiday one day. (less likely)
- We will go to London this year. (definite)
- We won't be living on the moon next month. (definitely not)
- You can book a holiday online. (probably will)
- You could book a holiday online. (probably won't)
- You must take a passport with you when you travel abroad. (External rule imposed by someone else, here the border control people.)

1. Add a suitable modal verb into these sentences. Remember to use a verb that states the possibility of something happening.

   a. Aunt Polly _____ come and visit us this weekend.

   b. We _____ go to the Galapagos Islands one day.

   c. I think we definitely _____ ever live on Mars.

   d. We _____ go and get the ice creams for the class.

   e. The driver told us we _____ wear seatbelts when we are on the bus.

Remember

We also use modals to ask for permission to do something. For example:

- *Can* I park my car here?
- You *must* buy a permit before mooring your boat for the night.
- We *will* have to pay a fine if we leave the coach here.

2. What kind of modal verb is being used in each sentence below? Put the letter **L** for likelihood; **N** for something necessary; and **P** for permission needed.

   a. We may go jogging in the park at the weekend.

   b. Can I borrow your ruler please?

   c. You must hand in your homework on Friday.

   d. We will get into trouble if we are late again.

   e. We might go and get you some sweets if you are good.

3. You are guiding some tourists around your local museum, but there are a few rules they need to know before you start. Tell them, using modal verbs, five rules they need to follow during the visit. For example:

   • You must leave your bags in the museum cloakroom.

   a. You may _____

   b. You must _____

   c. You will _____

   d. You won't _____

   e. You mustn't _____

4. At the end of the visit, you need to ask the tourists three questions before they leave. Using modals, ask them to do three things.

   a. Could you fill in your answers to this _____?

   b. Will you make sure you have _____?

   c. Can you please _____?

5. Complete the paragraph below, using modals, on how you would do the guided tour better next time.

   Next time, I *will* make sure we all meet in the green room. We *won't* meet in the foyer because it is too

   busy. I might ask James to _____ so I *can* give that to the tourists as well. I *might*

   charge them extra if they want to _____ I *should* _____ but I probably

   won't have time before the next tourist visit tomorrow.

Writing a travelogue

Guidance

You are going to write your own travelogue, but first let's have a look at some key elements and skills that help to create strong, descriptive writing. To bring a travelogue to life for others who haven't been to the place you are describing, you can use sensory, descriptive language. Sensory language appeals to the five senses: touch, sight, sound, smell and taste.

1. Let's first focus on sight. What does the location look like? Is it a building? Is it a mountain? Is it a field? Fill in the gaps to describe what this place might look like.

   > I was standing in the middle of a _____ I couldn't see anyone, but there was an
   >
   > _____ in the corner. There was a noise coming from the same area and I think the noise
   >
   > was coming from _____ Then all of a sudden, the noise stopped.

2. The sounds of a place can help bring it to life. What can these people hear? Is it music? Can they hear animals? Can they hear rain? Fill in the gaps below.

   > I could hear the _____ in the trees then suddenly they all stopped
   >
   > _____ Clouds had appeared and a few seconds later it was _____ the
   >
   > drops _____ on the ground.

3. Let's concentrate on touch. What does Peter feel in this short passage? Is it something soft? Is it something rough? It is something damp? Fill in the gaps below.

   > Peter could feel the _____ stones underfoot and was trying to move without making a
   >
   > sound. It had been raining all day, so his walking boots were _____ and he was careful
   >
   > not to slip. However, he did fall and when he hit the ground his hands felt _____.

4. Now have a go at a full paragraph, adding descriptive words for the sight, sound and touch of the place. Try to make it powerful, tense or exciting.

   > When Desmond got there, the street was empty. The only things moving were _____.
   >
   > He could hear _____ but he couldn't see any. The road felt _____ under
   >
   > his feet and he could smell the _____ as it had been raining that morning. He took a few
   >
   > steps, and heard the _____ underfoot. In the distance, he saw _____
   >
   > and after a few seconds realised they were coming closer. Desmond needed somewhere to hide. He heard
   >
   > _____ call out. He turned and ran towards the open door, _____ it shut
   >
   > just in time.

5. Look at the pictures. Which of these locations would you like to visit? Select one and then use sensory language to describe this place.

Your travelogue

Planning

1. Begin your travelogue by telling your readers exactly where you are. This part should be brief, but detailed enough to inform them. For example:

   ● I am in Paris, the capital of France, standing at an entrance to the Eiffel Tower, which is directly above me.

   Now write your opening sentence informing the reader where you are. You can be anywhere in the world.

   ----

2. You need to make the description more evocative, using one of the senses. For example:

   ● I can see several stalls, all selling hamburgers and hotdogs, and the aroma of freshly fried onions is filling the air.

   Write your next sentence, using one of the senses.

   ----

3. There must be a purpose – why are you there? Alistair and Leon were on an adventure, but our purpose is different. For example:

   ● I am here in Paris to learn more about 19th-century French art.

   Why are you where you are?

Teacher tip

It is up to you to use stronger sensory language to add more content. Make this as lively and entertaining as you can! You will be doing this in exercise 5 (on the next page), but before you do that you'll need to think about how to end your travelogue.

You could end your travelogue by writing what you feel you achieved that day. In our visit to Paris, for example:

● Today, I saw some amazing paintings at the Musee D'Orsay. They brought a chill to me, even though it was quite warm inside the gallery. I was so impressed.

4. How do you think you will end your travelogue?

Writing

5. Now use your plans and on a separate sheet of paper write a travelogue of your own. Aim to write about 150 words.

Skills checklist

When you have finished your travelogue, complete the following checklist.

? Have you used an appropriate register for your travelogue?

? Are the events you have written about in the order in which they happened?

? Have you used the continuous tense (past and present) in your travelogue?

? Have you used a range of sensory language? How many senses have you covered?

? Have you used strong words, to make readers feel as if they are there?

? Have you finished with an ending that sums up the day or the events?

Checking your progress

1. It is often said: "Travel broadens the mind." Write your own quote about what benefit you think travel has.

Grammar

2. Use the past continuous to complete the paragraph below.

   I ------------------------ to the travel agent when I saw a big advert telling me to visit Greece. I

   ------------------------ when my friend Charlie walked past. "Why don't we go?" said Charlie. "That

   was what I ------------------------" I said. We decided to book the holiday and the following week we

   were in Greece.

3. Using modal verbs, give three rules you might find when travelling on a boat.

   a. --

   b. --

   c. --

4. Using modal verbs, write down two things you must improve once you have completed this chapter.

   a. --

   b. --

5. Which relative pronouns would you add to the two sentences below?

   a. Alan is a train driver ----------------------- showed me how a steam train works.

   b. The steam train is amazing and ----------------------- is extremely powerful.

Writing

6. Which of these sentences would you find in a travelogue? Tick your answer.

   a. There is lower gravity on the moon than on earth.

   b. I am standing in a field and can see the sparkling stars clearly above me.

   c. Once you have baked the cake, allow it to cool before icing.

7. List some words to describe how the writer of a travelogue might *feel.*

----

8. You are standing on a beach. Write one sentence to describe what you can see.

----

9. You are travelling to work by train. Write down at least two things you can hear.

----

10. a. Now create your own question about modal verbs and ask a friend to answer it. You could ask about when it is appropriate to use a modal verb, or maybe not appropriate. For example, this doesn't sound correct:

● *You <u>must</u> travel to Mars on the proposed one-way journey in 2025.*

You could come up with a similar statement and ask your friend to use a more appropriate modal verb.

----

b. What have you found most useful in this chapter? In the boxes use three ticks for the most useful and one tick for the least useful!

● Using a range of modal verbs

● Using the past continuous accurately

● Getting to know relative pronouns better

● Developing my knowledge of sensory language

● Writing a paragraph of a travelogue

c. Which statement best describes you? Tick your response.

● *I know what a travelogue is, but struggle to use the five senses, the past continuous and a suitable register in my writing.*

● *I recognise how to use sensory language, the past continuous and the correct register, but find it hard to incorporate all of these techniques in my travelogues. continuous and the correct register, but find it hard to incorporate all of these techniques in my travelogues.*

● *I'm confident that I understand and can use the appropriate register, sensory language and past continuous to write purposeful and evocative travelogues.*

Leisure and entertainment

Imagine you are a famous director. You want to put on a play, but which one will you choose and where will you stage it? Write your ideas below.

The play I would stage would be

----

because

I would stage it at the

----

because

The Minack Theatre

In 1929, local drama enthusiasts … were looking for a **venue** to perform *The Tempest*.

Rowena Cade, who lived in Minack House [in Cornwall, England] decided that the cliffs below her garden would be the perfect **setting**, and … she and her gardener, Billy Rawlings, moved endless **granite** boulders and earth, creating the lower terraces of the theatre, much as they are today.

Although the Minack is built into huge granite cliffs, almost all of the theatre is made from concrete, mixed with local beach sand. Rowena carried many tons of sand…to the theatre where the concrete was used for seats, pillars, steps and walkways. Many of the seats in the theatre **bear** the name of a play or performance, each carefully carved into the wet concrete, and Rowena carved many intricate designs into new structures as they were made.

… Today's theatre **incorporates** the latest technology in lighting and sound, all controlled from a small room built into a rocky outcrop above the stage.

… The Minack attracts more than 80,000 playgoers every year as well as more than 150,000 visitors who come to look round during the day, but the atmosphere of this unique theatre still reflects the **vision** of its founder Rowena Cade, who created one of the world's most beautiful theatres.

Source: https://www.minack.com/our-history-1/

Building your vocabulary

venue: place where a pre-arranged and organised event takes place

setting: location or surroundings where an event takes place

granite: type of hard rock often used in building

bear: to carry

incorporates: includes

vision: future plan or idea

1. Where is the Minack Theatre?

    ----

2. Why was it built?

    ----

3. Why is much of the theatre made of concrete rather than natural granite?

    ----

4. What effect on the local area do you think the theatre has had?

    ----

5. The first play performed there was *The Tempest*. Why was this a good choice?

    ----

6. Explain why you would like to visit the Minack Theatre.

Prefixes

Looking closely

Prefixes can be added to the beginning of words and are used to modify the meaning of a word. For example, *multi* means *many* so adding the prefix *multi* to coloured will give *multi-coloured*, meaning *many coloured*.

Each prefix has the same meaning no matter which word it prefixes. Here are a few examples:

Prefix	Meaning	Examples
pre	before	prefix, pre-empt
post	after	postscript, postdate
co	with	cooperate, co-exist
de	negative	detox, dehumidifier
inter	mixed or between	international, interact
mini	small	minimarket, miniskirt

1. Write down five words you can make using the prefix *multi*.

   a. -------------------------------------

   b. -------------------------------------

   c. -------------------------------------

   d. -------------------------------------

   e. -------------------------------------

2. Underline the prefix in each of these three words.

   a. megastar

   b. unhappy

   c. polyglot

3. Now use each of the three words in exercise 2 to make three new sentences.

   a. ---

   b. ---

   c. ---

4. Draw lines to match each prefix to a suitable word. Then add each new word you've created to a sentence below.

inter		talented
super		net
mini		phone
multi		star
tele		bus

a. I booked the concert on the ------------------------------------.

b. As the performance started, my ------------------------------------ link failed, so I couldn't watch the play.

c. We will travel to the theatre by ------------------------------------.

d. The lead actor is a ------------------------------------.

e. The composer can also act; he is ------------------------------------.

5. Add a prefix from the box below to each word in brackets to complete the paragraph. Make sure you only use each prefix once.

| inter | multi | mini | tele |

I love art and I love colour, so it is only natural that my latest painting is ------------------------
(coloured). I drew a ------------------------ (sketch) first and then painted the larger one later. I have
sold a couple of paintings after they appeared on the ------------------------ (vision) and when I am
older, I hope to sell to an ------------------------ (national) market.

6. Choose two words from the examples in the 'Looking closely' box on page 90 and write two sentences using those words.

a. --

b. --

Teacher tip

Prefixes change the meaning of a word and carry the same general meaning each time they are added to a word because the reader and the writer both understand the meaning the prefix has. However, prefixes cannot be used on their own and do not have any meaning on their own.

Homonyms

Looking closely

Homonyms are words that are spelled the same way, but have a different meaning. Since homonyms have exactly the same spelling, it is more difficult when you are reading and writing to identify and use a homonym. Here are some examples of homonyms. Note that some of these have more than two alternative meanings:

- bank   *a place where money is kept* or *the side of a river*
- bark   *the covering of a tree* or *the sound a dog makes*
- match   *to be the same or similar to* or *another name for a sports game*

1. In each sentence below, the homonym has been underlined. Write a sentence below to show another meaning of the underlined word.

   a. Last year, he played Robin Hood and had a <u>bow</u> and arrow as props.

   ----

   b. In the interval, the cast had to <u>change</u> their costumes.

   ----

   d. At the end of the play, the opera star threw a <u>rose</u> into the audience.

   ----

2. Underline the homonym in each of the following sentences.

   a. I like to watch drama and comedies, but not tragedies.

   b. The programme was small and light.

3. Now write a sentence to show an alternative meaning of each homonym from exercise 2.

   a. --

   b. --

4. Write one sentence for each meaning of the homonyms below.

   a. cast

   ----

   b. club

Homophones

Looking closely

Some words are not spelled the same, but when you say them out loud they sound the same; these are called homophones. For example, *aloud* sounds the same as *allowed*, so you will need to work out which one is being used from the context, using context clues. Homophones are therefore more challenging when you are talking and listening than when you are reading and writing. Here are some examples of homophones:

flower/flour	hair/hare	night/knight
plain/plane	weight/wait	tale/tail

Some homophones can have several meanings. For example:

I'll	isle	aisle
to	two	too

1. Complete the sentences below using the appropriate homophone in brackets.

    a. The performance starts at _____ tonight. (ate/eight)

    b. We waited for the stage crew to _____ the curtain. (rays/raise)

    c. I wondered _____ you liked the theatre. (weather/whether)

2. Now create three sentences using each of the unused homophones in exercise 1. Try to stay with the theme of leisure and entertainment.

    a. _____

    b. _____

    c. _____

3. Write a sentence using each of the homophones below.

he'll	heel	heal

    a. _____

    b. _____

    c. _____

4. What is the homophone of each word listed below? Write it next to the word given.

    a. be _____   b. saw _____   c. time _____

Punctuation to slow down the reader

Looking closely

You use punctuation to make sentences easier to read and understand. Also, punctuation can slow down the reader and make the person think carefully about what is being said. There are several types of punctuation, for example a comma, semi-colon and dash.

A comma is used:

- to separate short items on a list
- to frame an indefinite clause
- before and after direct speech when it comes mid-sentence
- after greeting in a letter, both formal and informal
- before a question tag.

You can use the semi-colon:

- to separate lists that contain phrases
- before a subordinate clause, which is more usual in formal writing.

A dash is more informal. For instance, it can be used in a letter to a friend before a subordinate clause. For example:

- Thanks for the invite to your party – I would love to come.

1. Add five commas to the letter below.

> Dear Augusta
>
> I would love to come to your party. I will bring the balloons sweets and a football. Did you hear Danny? He said "I love football parties" and he doesn't know does he?
>
> See you soon
>
> Max

2. Rewrite and add one or more semi-colons to each of the sentences below.

   a. I like going to the theatre to see a pantomime each year but only before Christmas.

   ----

   b. We are taking: two large red rucksacks two canvas hammocks and two spare pairs of trainers.

   ----

c. I don't know what the weather will be like next month but we will go to the party anyway.

----

3. Add two commas and two semi-colons to the following short paragraph.

Each evening I like to go to the sports centre with my best friend of course! We do running swimming and lifting weights but the best part is the sauna afterwards.

4. Add a dash to these sentences.

a. I got your letter wow that is really exciting!

----

b. Violet went first hooray!

----

5. Add a comma and a dash to these sentences.

a. I will tell her Jia and Liang don't forget to bring the candles!

----

b. That's great now we just need the bread butter and apples.

Writing a review of a play

Guidance

A review of a play tells the reader about: the story; the main characters; the main actors; the director; the scenery and music; and whether the reviewer would recommend it or not. Written in semi-formal language, it often ends with a rating out of five.

When telling the reader about the play, begin with the name of the play and playwright, and perhaps where you saw it. Then give the setting of the play, the location and time of the action (the year, month, season or time of day the action takes place). Then write about the action, characters and other features (already listed).

In the final sentence or two you have to tell the reader whether you think the play is worth seeing. Make your opinions clear, for example:

- One of the best parts of the play is when …

However, sometimes you will be giving opinions that look more like facts, for example:

- The director … (chose a good cast/guided the actors well/has a clever overall vision of the play).

1. Look at the features in the list above, read the review below and then tick the features that appear.

   The Second Man is an interesting play about three men, Bill, Bob and Ben who are on a journey from Casablanca to Cape Town. Fred Jenner has written a masterpiece and the scenery was very clever as the stage moved around the car that the characters were in. I won't say which of the three men is the second man of the title, but I will say that it is a must-see production.

main characters	☐	what happens in the play	☐	playwright	☐
main actors	☐	director	☐	music	☐
scenery	☐	costumes	☐	recommendation	☐

2. Write down three adjectives you could use to describe the scenery of a play.

   a. --------------------   b. --------------------   c. --------------------

3. Complete the notes below about a play you have seen.

   Name of the play ------------------------   The play's location: ------------------------------

   Name of the playwright: --------------------   Period of the play: ------------------------------

4. Look at the features in the list below, read the review and then tick the features that appear in the review.

The Keeper by Harold Hackney is one of the finest plays written in modern times. The two main character are Mack and Ashton, middle-aged friends who are planning to steal some money. They want to escape their current dull lives and plan to build new lives in The Parks district of the capital, an affluent and trendy area. Will they succeed in the theft or will they ultimately be too cowardly to carry it out? Ian Burnley plays Mack and Patrick Mirfield plays Ashton, both fine actors giving believable performances here. When Ashton turns to Mack in tears at one point, it is hard to remember we are only watching a play, until the poignant music starts up and the curtain comes down at the end of the first half. I have to give this play five out of five.

name of play	☐	main characters	☐	director	☐
name of playwright	☐	rating	☐	scenery	☐
setting	☐	actors	☐	costumes	☐
time of play	☐	music	☐		

5. Write two sentences giving your opinion about a play you have seen. One sentence should use a phrase to make your opinion clear; the other should give an opinion that looks more like a fact.

a. One of the highlights was _____

_____

_____

b. The scenery, on the other hand, was _____

_____

_____

Your review

Planning

You are going to write a review of a play you have seen. You will write about 150 words recommending why readers should go and see the play, but first let's plan the review.

1. Look at these two sentences from play reviews. Tick the one you think is the most interesting.

   a. The play is set in New York, near the river, in a baker's where the main character works.

   b. The main character, a New York baker, does not know a secret at the start of the play; he does by the time it ends.

2. Use this exercise to plan your review.

   a. Write down the name of the play: _____

   b. Circle the type of play it is:

   comedy   tragedy   romance

   historical   mystery   thriller

   c. What happens to the main characters? Underline the idea you like the best.

   • They are on a journey.

   • They have seen something happen.

   • They are discussing something.

   d. Now add two details of what happens to the main characters.

   _____

   _____

   e. What did you think of the actors in the play?

   _____

   f. What was the music like? Underline one from each pair below.

   • original/cover version

   • live/pre-recorded

   g. Write one word to describe what you thought of the play.

   _____

Guidance

Now you are going to write your review. Here is a format you can follow:

- Give the name of the play and the playwright.

- Name the main two or three characters who are central to the play.

- Give a brief plot outline, without giving away the ending of the play.

- State how convincing the main actors are in the play.

- State how realistic the costumes are.

- State whether the music was an original composition or used well-known music and whether this was the right choice for the play.

Remember that you will need to include your final opinion of the play at the end and then give a rating out of five stars for what you have seen.

Writing

3. You have recently been to the theatre and seen a play, which you would like to recommend to the readers of a local magazine. Use the ideas and skills you have practised in this chapter, and on a separate sheet of paper write a review of the play in about 150 words.

Skills checklist

When you have finished your review, complete the following checklist.

? Have you included the name of the play and the main characters?

? Have you given a brief outline of the plot?

? Have you used semi-formal language?

? Have you encouraged the reader to go and see it?

? Have you given your honest opinions?

? Have you written an interesting review?

Checking your progress

1. In William Shakespeare's play, *All's Well That Ends Well,* Jaques says *"All the world's a stage, And all the men and women merely players."* Write your own quote about the theatre.

Grammar

2. What meaning does the prefix *post* carry when it is affixed to another word? Give an example.

   ----

3. Add a word with a prefix to complete this sentence.

   When he was younger, he was only known in his country, but when he was older, the actor's fame

   was --------------------.

4. Write two sentences that give two meanings of the word *wound*.

   a. --

   ----

   b. --

   ----

5. Add the correct punctuation to the sentence below to slow the reader down.

   The playwright said he needed a good idea some paper and a pen to write with and a fresh cup of coffee.

Writing

6. Write down three events you could write a review about.

   a. --

   b. --

   c. --

7. Write down three areas you might focus on when writing a play review.

   a. --

   b. --

   c. --

8. Complete this play review adding adjectives to give the reviewer's opinion.

The lead actor, Amrish Kumar, gave a ------------------- performance and the other lead,

Romesh Rampal, was -------------------. The writing was ------------------- and the director was

clearly very -------------------. Overall, this play was -------------------.

9. Complete this section of a review about the costumes and scenery of a play.

The play is set in 1875, but the scenery makes it look like -------------------. The costumes

are ------------------- and most of them are made of -------------------. The costumes look

------------------- for the actor to wear.

10. Now it is time to make an evaluation of your progress through this chapter. Circle your response.

   a. How confident are you when:

• *Using prefixes?*	very	quite	sometimes	not very	I need help
• *Using commas, semi-colons and dashes?*	very	quite	sometimes	not very	I need help
• *Using homonyms and homophones?*	very	quite	sometimes	not very	I need help

   b. Which statement best describes you? Tick your response.

      • *I know what a review is, but struggle to write a clear review.*

      • *I recognise the key features used in a review, but find it hard to incorporate them all into my reviews.*

      • *I'm confident that I understand how to write reviews and can use my knowledge to produce an effective review.*

   c. Write a sentence without commas, semi-colons or a dash and then ask someone else to punctuate it.

If you were choosing a hobby or interest to begin what quality would be most important to you?

| The thrill of taking part | What I create | What I achieve |

The quality I would find most important is

----

because

Get out there and go for it!

I don't over-egg the pudding when I say that everyone needs a hobby or interest; something **constructive** and **fulfilling** to eat up those spare hours between work and sleep. Your own little goldmine of personal satisfaction that defines you as the person you really are. Me? I'm proud to say I am a model kit maker. I build **complex** scale models of everything from classic cars to **reproductions** of legendary steam locomotives. No matter that I've built hundreds of these models over thousands of hours, I still get butterflies in my stomach when I enter my favourite model shop on my quest for the next project. There is something wonderfully exciting about diving into the box of a newly purchased kit for the first time, spreading out the **components** on the work table and studiously **surveying** the instructions. I'm a kid in a candy store with no fear of the dentist's chair.

Now, I know that building model kits isn't everyone's cup of tea, but it really doesn't matter what hobby or interest you choose because everyone's different. Just don't be a couch potato. Don't sit on the fence any longer. Get out there and choose your poison. You won't regret it!

Building your vocabulary

constructive:	positive and good
fulfilling:	satisfying
complex:	made up of many parts
reproductions:	copies
component:	each of the parts something is made up of
surveying:	carefully inspecting

1. What is a complex model?

   ----

2. Underline the two reasons why hobbies and interests are good for you.

   a. They are constructive and fulfilling ways to spend your spare time.

   b. They are easy to do and not expensive.

   c. A hobby such as building complex reproductions is very satisfying.

   d. They require little time and effort.

3. Why would surveying the instructions before starting be a good idea? Explain your answer.

   ----

4. How necessary is it for a model maker to recognise all the component parts in a kit being built?

   ----

5. The writer uses a number of idioms, such as *over-egg the pudding*, in his article together with abbreviations, such as *I'm* and *won't*, to create an informal style. How does this style help to put the message across?

   ----

6. If you were helping a friend to choose a new hobby, what advice would you give?

Idioms

Remember

An idiom is a phrase in which the meaning cannot be explained by just reading it. It is an image that only makes sense if both the writer and the reader understand the intended context and the idea behind it. Idioms are normally used in more informal writing to create interest.

Teacher tip

In the article on page 102, the writer has used a number of idioms. The title itself is an idiom:

- Get out there and go for it!

The literal meaning is vague and asks more questions than it answers. For instance:

- Where is *out there*?

- Where are you being asked to *go*?

- What is it that you are being told to *go for*?

The phrase only makes sense if you understand the context in which it is being used. In this case it means: *Be positive and do something.*

1. The following are idioms used in the article. Match each one to its intended meaning in the box below. The first one is done for you.

don't over exaggerate	become excited	really happy
eagerly explore	full of riches	lazy inactive person
enjoy so much it goes quickly		

   a. don't over egg the pudding   means   *don't over exaggerate*

   b. eat up   means   --------------------------------

   c. goldmine   means   --------------------------------

   d. butterflies in my stomach   means   --------------------------------

   e. diving into   means   --------------------------------

   f. kid in a candy store   means   --------------------------------

   g. couch potato   means   --------------------------------

2. There are two more idioms in the last paragraph. Explain their meaning.

   a. ---

   ----

   b. ---

Euphemisms

Looking closely

A euphemism is a word or phrase used in place of one that is likely to cause upset. Euphemisms can replace a word or term when it is not acceptable to use the correct one. For example:

- Instead of saying someone has died the euphemism *passed away* is used.

Sometimes euphemisms are used to soften meaning by using humour. For example:

- *To bite the dust* is used to mean to die, to fall over or to end in failure.

Unlike idioms, euphemisms usually hold a clue to their meaning in the word or phrase used.

3. Tick the correct meaning for each of these euphemisms.

   a. The euphemism *being let go* really means:

   | being sacked from a job | ◯ | being an important person | ◯ | being pushed away | ◯ |

   b. The basketball player was *vertically challenged* really means he was:

   | good at jumping | ◯ | too short | ◯ | didn't like heights | ◯ |

   c. If someone is called the salt of the earth, this really means:

   | they are unfriendly | ◯ | they like the outdoors | ◯ | they are very nice and trustworthy | ◯ |

4. Now it is time for you to have some fun playing with words. Create your own euphemism for each of the following ideas.

   a. Someone playing a violin badly.

   ----

   b. Defending a bad decision you have made.

   ----

   c. Telling a friend he or she is wrong about something.

Teacher tip

When is it acceptable to use idioms and euphemisms? Try not to use them in formal pieces of writing such as reports. If you are writing a story or a more informal piece then use them, but be careful that the intended meaning is correct. Look out for examples and try to work out their meaning.

Emphasis words

Looking closely

Sometimes it is not enough to simply describe an action or situation; it is necessary to add emphasis to the statement to make it stand out or express the strength of feeling intended. In these cases, emphatic words should be used to stress the importance of the idea.

Hyperbole is a device used to create an effect based on exaggeration. The idea is to stress the point being made by exaggerating the situation. It is often used in a humorous context, but can also be used to show anger and frustration. For example:

- "Mandip, I've told you a *thousand times* that I don't like stamp collecting!" shouted Sara.

In this example, Sara is frustrated and exaggerates how many times she has said she doesn't like stamp collecting, to stress the point to Mandip.

1. For each example below, explain what effect the use of hyperbole is trying to create. The first one is done for you.

   a. This band makes the best music ever!

      This is my favourite band.

   b. Skateboarding is a million times cooler than cycling.

      ----

   c. The cricketer hit the ball into orbit.

      ----

   d. These dance shoes are killing me.

      ----

   e. After running a marathon I drank gallons of water.

      ----

2. Underline the nine examples of hyperbole in the following passage.

   Moving faster than the speed of light, screaming like the crowd at a pop concert, with my heart racing at a thousand beats to the second, I feel through the air to complete my bungee jump challenge. Miles below the raging torrents of the river awaited any mistake. I felt as heavy as an elephant yet light as a feather as I bounced up and down held only by the cotton thread attached to my ankle. I was as petrified as an ancient forest, but at the same time happier than anyone on the planet because I had done it; the challenge was completed.

Weak and strong words

Looking closely

Some words are used in general terms to suggest an action or state. Using a more specific word can make your writing more effective.

For example, the verb *went* is a good example of a word that can be replaced by a better choice.

Instead of 'I *went* to the forest to practise my map-reading skills' try one of the following:

- I drove along a dusty track to the forest …
- I cycled through the rain to the forest …
- I walked two miles to the forest …

In each example more interest and accuracy has been added.

3. In each of the sentences below, replace *went* with a better verb. Make sure you use a different one each time.

a. We all *went* on our favourite ride at the theme park yesterday.

----

b. Jared *went* to the scuba diving centre as it was a Saturday afternoon.

----

c. They all *went* to the cinema to watch the latest movie.

----

d. I love taking pictures so I *went* to the photography exhibition at my school.

----

4. The sentences below contain some more weak words that can be replaced to make your writing stronger. Rewrite the sentences and replace the underlined words with a better choice.

a. The meeting is <u>about</u> to start.

The meeting will start immediately.

b. The apple was <u>bad</u> so I threw it away.

----

c. I thought the art exhibition was <u>good</u>.

----

d. The flower display was very <u>nice</u>.

----

e. The instructions for building the model ship were <u>okay</u> and easy to follow.

----

f. <u>Quite</u> a crowd assembled to hear the band play.

Rhetorical devices

Looking closely

A rhetorical device is one used by a writer to persuade the reader to think about the point being made in the way the writer wants. Rhetorical devices can also create an emotional response by making the reader feel a certain way about the subject being discussed.

A rhetorical question is one where the answer is suggested in the question. This type of question is used to persuade readers to believe what the writer wants them to. For example:

- You don't really want to buy another model aircraft kit, do you? (Here we expect the answer to be no.)

Epizeuxis is the repeating of the same word for emphasis. For instance:

- I just love, love, love to dance.

1. Rhetorical questions often require only a *yes* or *no* answer. Provide yes or no responses below. The first one is done for you.

   a. Do you really have time to complete that model now? _____No_____

   b. Will you stop playing that game and come to dinner immediately? _____

   c. Aren't you tired of spending so much time in this model shop? _____

   d. Surely you don't expect me to agree to that request? _____

2. Circle the use of epizeuxis in each of these examples.

   a. No, no, no, I will not give up trying to learn this piano piece.

   b. I am not going to agree with you, ever, ever, ever!

   c. Oh, how horrible, how horrible it is when you hit the wrong note.

Looking closely

Anaphora is the repetition of a word or phrase at the beginning of successive clauses. For example:

- This flexing of muscles, this straining of tendons, this burning of energy we call dance is my greatest gift.

The repetition of *this* at the beginning of each clause stresses the importance. Here is another example:

- I dream of acting on stage. I dream of playing Shakespeare. I dream of endless applause.

Antithesis is when two opposite ideas are placed together to form a contrast. Shakespeare used it in *Hamlet*. For example:

- "Give *every man* thy ear, but *few* thy voice."

This means listen to everyone, but only speak to those you trust.

3. Underline the use of anaphora in each of the following.

a. Classical music is powerful, classical music is vibrant, classical music is open to everyone.

b. When I paint I feel alive, when I paint I feel free, but most of all when I paint I am me.

c. I remember my first dance lesson clearly. I remember the strict voice of the teacher and I remember the feeling of joy when I danced my first steps.

4. At the beginning of *A Tale of Two Cities* Charles Dickens tries to show the confusion in Europe at that time by using antithesis. Find Dickens' use of antithesis in the following paragraph and write your answers below. The first one is done for you.

It was the best of times, it was the worst of times, it was the age of wisdom, it was the age of foolishness, it was the epoch of belief, it was the epoch of incredulity, it was the season of Light, it was the season of Darkness, it was the spring of hope, it was the winter of despair, we had everything before us, we had nothing before us, we were all going direct to Heaven, we were all going direct the other way.

a. It was the best of times   contrasts with   it was the worst of times

b. it was the age of *wisdom*   contrasts with   ----------------------------

c. ----------------------------   contrasts with   it was the epoch of incredulity

d. it was the season of *Light*   contrasts with   ----------------------------

e. ----------------------------   contrasts with   ----------------------------

f. ----------------------------   contrasts with   ----------------------------

g. ----------------------------   contrasts with   ----------------------------

Teacher tip

There are many rhetorical devices that create different effects in your writing if used correctly. They are also powerful tools used by public speakers to persuade an audience. Do some research to find and understand the following types: analogy, oxymoron, metanoia and parallelism.

Writing a persuasive talk

People take up hobbies for different reasons. What do you think?

- My hobby excites me and makes me feel alive.
- When doing my hobby I feel relaxed and forget about real life.
- My hobby is just something to do when I am bored.

I think hobbies are _____

because _____

You are writing to persuade the audience that your viewpoint is the correct one so you do not need to consider both sides of the argument.

Guidance

Bias is a feeling or opinion that strongly favours one side of the argument over the other.

Here are two biased, but opposite opinions about stamp collecting:

Philately (stamp collecting) is a fascinating hobby that anyone can do and all will enjoy.

How can anyone think that sticking stamps in a book is anything other than boring and dull?

uses the correct term for the hobby to give a serious tone

fascinating is stronger than interesting

anyone and *all* suggest everyone can do it

boring and dull are both negative

uses a rhetorical question

sticking stamps is meant to be insulting

1. Decide whether the following statements are biased for or against the hobby of stamp collecting. The first one is completed for you.

    a. It is a hobby for rich people with lots of spare money. _____Against_____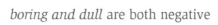

    b. This hobby is the best medicine for those who can't sleep at night. _____

    c. The most wonderful feature of stamps is their endless variety. _____

    d. Never has one hobby offered so much excitement and possibility. _____

    e. Do you want action, thrills, passion? This isn't for you. _____

    f. Escape into your own world of romantic adventures and thrilling stories. _____

2. Write two statements about your favourite hobby. One should be biased in favour of (or 'for' the hobby) and the other should be biased against the hobby.

    a. For: _____

    _____

    _____

    b. Against: _____

    _____

    _____

3. Including certain words and phrases in your talk will persuade your audience that what you say is correct. Complete the sentences using positive words and phrases from the box. There is more than one option for some of the gaps. Choose which you prefer.

I am sure you will agree	superior in every way	who wouldn't want to try
obviously without doubt of course		I firmly believe must
everybody knows that as you can clearly see		most definitely

    a. _____ this is the best hobby in the world!

    b. You _____ try this hobby. It is the _____ fun you will have in your spare time.

    c. Everything about this hobby is wonderful. It is _____ to anything else you can choose.

    d. _____ you won't find a more interesting hobby to try.

    e. I _____ recommend this hobby to you as _____ such an exciting and thrilling activity?

Teacher tip

The examples of positive words and phrases in the list above all work by persuading the audience that your viewpoint is the correct one. The use of rhetorical devices creates these powerful effects. Compile your own mini dictionary of imperatives and superlatives to use in your persuasive writing. Include them in your writing to practise your new vocabulary and skills.

Crafting a persuasive talk

Planning

You are going to prepare a five-minute talk on a hobby.

A well-crafted talk is one that:

- engages the audience in the first few sentences

- make a series of persuasive points using a range of rhetorical devices

- leaves the audience with a powerful message that is emphasised in the concluding statement.

1. Choose a hobby to talk about. Use the bullets below to map five main points between the introduction and conclusion. Each one is going to be a separate paragraph. Concentrate on the reasons why your hobby is so good. It doesn't matter about the order of your points yet.

Introduction

- ---

- ---

- ---

- ---

- ---

Conclusion

2. Once you are satisfied your points are strong and persuasive you need to organise them into a suitable order. Do this by adding a number from 2 to 6 next to each of your points above. (The introduction is number 1 and the conclusion is number 7.)

3. Your opening paragraph must grab the attention of the audience, so it must be lively, engaging and exciting. Which one of these two openings is the most effective? Write down your choice and reason below.

  a. I have been collecting superhero figures for five years. I have about five hundred and really like them. I read magazines about them and go to toy fairs. They can be worth quite a lot of money. I keep them safely in their boxes and never take them out, so they never get damaged.

  b. Imagine. You enter the store. Your eyes search every distant corner. Your heart is racing, your "must have" list is clutched in your trembling hand and your thoughts are pleading "please be here". Then you see it. You float across the floor in a dream; you reach for that most valued of boxes desperately hoping it isn't an illusion; you have it firmly in your sweaty grasp. It's yours. One mint condition limited edition highly prized Batman figure. Now who's the superhero?

I believe ----------------------- is the most effective because --

----

----

4. Ending with a strong persuasive comment is very important as it is the last detail your audience will remember.

    a. Why is the following ending not very effective?

        So, to conclude, collecting superhero figures is my favourite hobby. I find it very interesting and I think you will too.

        ----

    b. How is the ending below more effective?

        So let loose your inner superhero. Journey into a world where reality is suspended and imagination is unlimited. Feel the force, wrap your cape around you, be in touch with your superpowers and, without doubt, join me in this life-changing experience.

Writing

5. Now use your plans and on a separate sheet of paper write a five-minute persuasive talk that answers the following question:

- Why should you try my hobby?

Skills checklist

When you have finished your persuasive talk, complete the following checklist.

? Have you started with an engaging introduction and ended with a persuasive concluding comment? ☐

? Have you used bias effectively to put over your point of view? ☐

? Have you used a good range of rhetorical devices accurately? ☐

? Have you used a range of persuasive words and phrases to good effect? ☐

? Have you prepared enough material to last five minutes? ☐

Checking your progress

1. Sukant Ratnakar wrote: "Hobbies are like flowers on a plant. They make the plant look beautiful and feel proud." Write a quote that sums up how you feel about your favourite hobby or interest.

Grammar

2. On reading an incorrect answer, a teacher says: "It is a good effort but not quite what I had in mind."

   What is this an example of? Tick your answer.

   Metaphor ⬭ Euphemism ⬭ Idiom ⬭

3. Read the statement below (containing two idioms) and underline the intended meanings.

   • When starting a new hobby it is important to dip your toe in the water as quickly as possible before you get cold feet.

   a. *dip your toe in the water* means:

   don't be shy   wait patiently   make an attempt

   b. *get cold feet* means:

   suffer from bad circulation   become too scared to carry on   fall ill

4. Which of the following sentences are examples of hyperbole? Underline your answers.

   a. I'd walk a thousand miles to see my favourite band.

   b. How many times do I have to tell you I am not interested in your hobby?

   c. Even if I have to crawl on my hands and knees I will reach the top of the mountain.

5. Underline the use of anaphora in this passage.

   > I am sure you will agree that my hobby is the most important. I am sure you will come to believe that collecting stamps is much more important than playing video games. I am sure you will accept that what I do is combine geography and history to learn valuable lessons about our world. What you do is spend endless hours glued to a screen fighting pointless wars. What you do is waste endless hours achieving nothing. What you do is pointless.

Writing

6. Put the following opening statements in order with the most effective being number 1 and the least being 3.

   a. If you want to do something exciting then you have to try my hobby. ⬭

   b. My hobby is really interesting and you may like it too. ⬭

   c. Are you bored? Do you seek excitement? Is your life lacking direction? If the answer is yes to these questions do not fear for I have the perfect solution. ⬭

7. Which of these is not an example of bias? Tick your answer.

    a. Whoever says that collecting superhero figures is boring doesn't understand how exciting it is. ☐

    b. Collecting toy figures is childish and no hobby for a mature and intelligent teenager. ☐

    c. It is completely up to you whether you collect superhero figures or not. Everyone has different interests and all are equally valid. ☐

8. For each of the statements below, underline the more powerful word or phrase.

    a. Making scale models is a (*fascinating/quite good/okay*) hobby for all ages.

    b. (*I think you should try/I find it really hard to believe you haven't tried*) such an extremely exciting hobby.

    c. I can assure you (*beyond question/with some confidence/maybe*) that if you take up this hobby it will (*be life changing/be something to do/occupy your time*).

9. Rewrite the following passage to make it a more effective conclusion.

These reasons that I have stated are the ones why you should try my hobby. I think you will enjoy it so at least give it a go and then decide. I've had quite a few really interesting experiences while following my hobby and maybe you can have some too. Either way I'm going to continue doing what I like.

----

10. Now it is time to make an evaluation of your progress through this chapter. Circle your response.

    a. How confident are you when:

• *Using idioms and euphemism?*	very	quite	sometimes	not very	I need help
• *Creating hyperbole?*	very	quite	sometimes	not very	I need help
• *Using rhetorical devices?*	very	quite	sometimes	not very	I need help

    b. Which statement below best describes you? Tick your response.

        • *I find it hard to make my writing persuasive.* ☐

        • *I understand how persuasive writing works, but it is hard to write my view convincingly.* ☐

        • *I am confident that I can correctly use persuasive devices to convince my audience of my view.* ☐

    c. Write a question of your own about how to write a persuasive piece. Have an answer ready and try it out on someone you know.

----

9 Customs and cultures

How important are your customs and culture to you and why?

> They teach me who I am

> They connect me to my ancestors

> They're not relevant

Examples of customs in my culture are _____

_____

They are important because _____

_____

A cultural welcome to Hawaii

Welcome to Hawaii. My given Polynesian name is Ahohako, but you can call me by my everyday name, Rick. After all, we're living in the 21st century, right? I have lived in this **paradise** called Oahu all my life as my ancestors have for many generations. Where else would I want to go? I speak to you in English but in my other language, the language that sits **nagging** in my brain, Ahohako means 'storm'. I guess my parents knew what I'd be like as I was growing up!

Today this city of Honolulu is home to about 400 000 people and is a **bustling** centre for tourism and business alike but still there are those among us who cling **ferociously** to our history when life was more simple and rewarding. It was a time when farming, fishing and hunting were our way of life. A time when we lived in traditional grass huts in small villages where everyone knew each other and there was a real sense of working together as a community. A time when we were at one with our customs and our island, when the songs we sang were of brave warriors, and the custom we followed was kapu, meaning **taboo**. Now, my new friends, I will leave you with our traditional greeting and wish you a wonderful stay in our island paradise. Aloha.

Building your vocabulary

paradise:	a perfect place	**ferociously:**	fiercely
nagging:	painfully bothering	**taboo:**	a strict rule that forbids certain actions
bustling:	busy in an exciting way		

1. What is Rick's Polynesian name?

----

2. Underline the two reasons why life was easier for Rick's ancestors.

    a. Honolulu was a bustling city.

    b. Farming, fishing and hunting were more simple activities.

    c. People lived in small villages and knew each other.

    d. Hawaii was a long way from any other islands.

3. Why does Rick "*cling ferociously*" to his ancestors' history and cultural beliefs?

----

4. How does the use of the word "*paradise*" show what Rick thinks of his island home?

----

5. Although Rick speaks English every day, why might his knowledge of the Polynesian language be nagging in his brain?

----

6. If you were writing a list of rules based on a taboo system, what three things would you forbid?

Implication or inference

Remember

Implication and inference are opposites. An implication is used to suggest something in an indirect way without actually saying what is meant. When an inference is made the meaning is guessed at based on the evidence available. Usually the evidence used contains hints that allow an inference to take place.

1. The word group for *implication* also includes the following.

imply   implied   implies   implying

Underline the correct form of the word to complete the sentences below.

a. The writer (*implied/implication/implying*) that he had always loved Hawaii.

b. On leaving Hawaii, the (*implication/imply/implying*) was that he would be back soon.

c. If I am (*implying/imply/implication*) that I am a fan of Oahu then that is correct.

d. I did not mean to (*implication/implied/imply*) that Hawaii is too far away to visit.

e. Returning to Hawaii (*implies/implying/implied*) that I love this island.

2. In the passage on page 116, Rick says that he has lived on the island of Oahu all his life and asks the rhetorical question: "*Where else would I want to go?*" Although he doesn't say it directly, this implies that Rick thinks Oahu is the best place to live. Which of the following statements are also implied by Rick's question? Circle your answers.

a. Oahu is a perfect place to live.   Yes/No

b. The world is a big, scary place.   Yes/No

c. Everyone should want to live on Oahu.   Yes/No

d. Oahu is the biggest island in the state of Hawaii.   Yes/No

e. Oahu will always be Rick's home.   Yes/No

Looking closely

When trying to remember the difference between an implication and an inference, it is important to remember which comes first. An implication can often lead to an inference, but not the other way around. For example:

● Implication: My Polynesian language is nagging in my brain.

● Inference: I want to speak in Polynesian instead of English.

Although his real given name is Ahohako, Rick tells his guests to call him by his everyday name instead. This *implies* that he chooses not to use his Polynesian name and infers:

● He doesn't like his real name.

● It is a special name he doesn't want strangers to use.

Since an inference is a guess based on what evidence is available, both of these points could be true.

3. The word group for *inference* also includes the following.

> infer   inferring   inferred

Underline the correct form of the word to complete these sentences.

a. I can (*inferring/infer/inferred*) from your statement that Honolulu is a busy city.

b. If you are (*inferring/inferred/inference*) that I am a lover of culture you are correct.

c. An (*infer/inferring/inference*) can be made as a result of an implication.

d. When you (*inferred/inference/inferring*) that you were sad to leave Hawaii I knew you liked it.

4. Match the inference to the statement. Write your answers on the lines provided.

- We must make sure our old ways and customs survive.
- We must make sure our language is taught to the young.
- The younger generation must not forget our customs as young people are the future.
- Polynesian is not being spoken enough by the majority of our people.
- Our lives in the past were better.

a. I would choose fishing, hunting and farming over tourism any day.

----

b. Ferociously we defend our old ways and customs.

----

c. How often do we hear Polynesian being spoken on Oahu?

----

d. It is important for the younger generation to remember their ancestors' customs.

----

e. I fear that in 50 years' time no Polynesian languages will be spoken by our children.

Antonyms

> ## Remember
>
> An antonym is a word with the opposite meaning to another given word. *In* and *out* are antonyms of each other as they have opposite meanings.
>
> Antonyms should not be confused with synonyms (which are words that have similar meanings) or homonyms (which is the collective noun for homophones and homographs).

1. Look at this sentence:

   - I tried to book a <u>direct</u> flight to Honolulu airport, but I could only get an <u>indirect</u> one instead.

In this example *indirect* is the antonym of *direct* as they are opposites. Underline the antonyms in the sentences below.

   a. Coffee has a bitter taste unlike pineapple which has a sweet taste.

   b. The days are hot in Hawaii and the nights are never cold.

   c. Hawaiian fishermen were brave and skilful, none were cowardly or unskilled.

   d. The most successful warriors were strong, but unsuccessful warriors were weak.

2. Which of these pairs are antonyms of each other? Circle your answers.

a.	visible	invisible	Yes/No
b.	valuable	invaluable	Yes/No
c.	fearless	frightened	Yes/No
d.	young	old	Yes/No
e.	rich	poor	Yes/No

> ## Looking closely
>
> The meaning of a sentence can be changed to the opposite by the use of just one word. For example:
>
> - I am really impressed by the skill displayed by a Polynesian fire-eater.
>
> *This becomes:*
>
> - I am really <u>not</u> impressed by the skill displayed by a Polynesian fire-eater.
>
> Sometimes it is more complicated than just adding one word to change the meaning of a sentence. For example:
>
> - I <u>went</u> to the luau last night and I <u>thoroughly enjoyed</u> all the singing and dancing.
>
> *This becomes:*
>
> - I <u>didn't go</u> to the luau last night so I <u>didn't enjoy</u> all the singing and dancing.

3. Change each sentence below to make it mean the opposite.

    a. I really did enjoy the day I spent at the heritage centre in Honolulu.

    ----

    b. I will be excited when it's my turn to try steering the outrigger.

    ----

    c. I cannot believe how powerful Hawaiian chieftains were in the past.

    ----

    d. I shall remember my time at the Hawaiian village and the skills that were on show.

    ----

4. Rewrite this paragraph by changing its meaning to the opposite.

> A luau, a traditional Hawaiian evening of food and entertainment, is everybody's favourite way to spend a night on Oahu. It is full of high-quality performers and isn't at all a tourist trap. An evening spent under the stars will give lasting memories and will show you much about the Polynesian culture on the island.

Teacher tip

The best place to check whether a word is an antonym is in a thesaurus, which lists both synonyms and antonyms of words. A quick exercise is to choose any ten adjectives at random and then try to work out their antonyms. Use a thesaurus to see whether you were correct.

Choosing words in context

Looking closely

Verbs and adjectives can be positive, neutral or negative. Carefully chosen words can create a specific tone in writing to make the reader feel an emotional response. The context that is created makes a big difference to how a piece of writing is read and understood.

Using positive words creates a good feeling in a piece of writing, but only works if the context is correct. For instance:

- So much natural beauty makes Hawaii a paradise.

1. Read this passage about Hawaii's greatest king. Underline the positive words.

> King Kamehameha is generally considered to be Hawaii's greatest king. He was a brave and talented warrior, strong and resourceful in battle and wise and honourable when ruling the islands. He united the islands and made them rich, peaceful and prosperous. He was a good diplomat and cared greatly for his people.

2. Here is a list of words that describe being happy. Use at least five of them to write a short description of a time when you were very happy.

cheerful	delighted	glad	grateful
hopeful	overjoyed	pleased	thrilled

Looking closely

Using negative words creates a bad feeling in a piece of writing, but can be very effective if the context calls for this tone. The underlined words below create the negative tone.

> Far from being perfect, Hawaii is in constant danger of deadly hurricanes, erupting volcanoes, destructive floods and terrible tsunamis. Toxic carbon dioxide clouds and fierce lava flows are also a serious threat to the islanders.

This paints a different, more negative picture so it wouldn't be a good idea to put it in a tourist information brochure. However, it could be appropriate in the context of a scientific study or a newspaper article.

3. The paragraph below describes King Kamehameha in a more negative context. Underline the negative words used to do this.

> King Kamehameha was a ruthless warrior who killed hundreds of his enemies in blood-soaked battles. He was heartless in his selfish desire to force all the islanders to kneel fearfully beneath his iron will.

4. Negative words are often used to criticise people or places. Rewrite each sentence in a negative tone. The first one is done for you.

a. The clean and sparkling beach was alive with the sound of happy children playing in the glistening sand.

The dirty oil-stained beach was polluted with the deafening noise of badly behaved children arguing in the litter-strewn sand.

b. The clean, tidy school bus was filled with excited children happily on their way to the amazing museum.

----

c. The eager school children listened attentively to the wonderful lesson about their country's fascinating customs.

----

d. The tasty lunch provided by the thoughtful museum staff was the best the children had ever been lucky enough to experience on a school trip.

Teacher tip

As well as positive and negative words there are also neutral words. These can be used when a more measured and less emotional tone is required. Neutral words can be used to write balanced pieces that aim to be fair and free of opinion. Do some research to create a bank of ten neutral words you can use in your writing.

Writing an article

Writing about others' points of view and cultures can be very difficult. What do you think?

- It is hard to write fairly about points of view I disagree with and cultures I don't really understand.

- I prefer to write about my own points of view and culture.

- I think it's easy because I'm really interested in others' viewpoints and cultures.

Writing about others' viewpoints and cultures is _____

because _____

_____

You are going to plan and write an article about understanding others' points of view and cultures.

Guidance

Just like using positive or negative words, using neutral words can set a tone and be very effective. Using neutral words creates a calm and measured tone.

A traditional Hawaiian hut can be described in a negative tone as:

- <u>small</u> and <u>empty</u> with <u>little natural light</u>, <u>no furniture</u> and a <u>roof made of grass</u>.

A more measured neutral tone would describe the hut as:

- functional with a thatched roof and a floor covered by woven mats and little furniture as Hawaiians traditionally sat on the floor.

This neutral version just describes the hut without making a judgment about its condition or traditions.

Implication is normally used to express opinion in writing so that an inferred meaning is clear, such as:

- Why would anyone ever want to climb a tree without a safety harness?

The question is rhetorical as the implied meaning suggests the writer finds this activity dangerous. The reader, therefore, can infer that the writer thinks the activity is dangerous and foolish.

Another more neutral way to express this point would be as follows:

- Climbing a tree without a safety harness could be considered a dangerous activity.

The implication that you shouldn't do it is still present, but it is written less negatively.

1. Which of the sentences below is more neutral and less judgmental? Tick your answer.

   a. The traditional Hawaiian way of life was limited and basic.

   b. Traditional life in a Hawaiian village was full of laughter, song and people obviously at one with their lives and nature.

   c. Traditional Hawaiian life centred on a village community based on farming, fishing and hunting.

2. Rewrite the following paragraph using neutral words to create a neutral tone.

> Tree climbing has been a scary tradition in Hawaii for centuries, which is much too long. Whatever possesses these crazy people to climb bare-footed and with only a thin strand of rope precariously tied around their ankles is beyond me. Why do they do this? Just to get a coconut! Regarded as a brave and manly skill, I call it foolhardy.

----

3. Rewrite the opinions below to include the implication, but using a more neutral tone. The first one is done for you.

a. I am at a loss to understand why climbing a tree is considered such a huge skill.

Climbing a tree is considered a skill.

b. Why so many people go to watch the annual professional tree-climbing competition on Oahu amazes me.

----

c. Coconuts have long been a staple food on the island, but would you like to live near a tree that drops heavy fruits from a great height at regular intervals?

----

d. There is always the feeling with coconuts that it takes a lot of effort to pick and open them before you get to the best part.

Your article

Planning

You are going to plan and write an article about understanding others' points of view and cultures.

An approach where the writer uses implication to offer opinions can cause offence to some readers, but it doesn't have to if the writing is carefully crafted. This means that the writer has planned the piece to be thoughtful and informative without being full of opinions that only see one side of an argument.

An example of a statement that isn't crafted and could cause offence is as follows:

- The Hawaiian system of taboo was a primitive attempt at creating a peaceful community based on strict rules.

The use of *primitive* suggests unsophisticated and basic and this creates a negative tone that could insult Hawaiians who have great pride in their ancestors. A more crafted statement would be:

- The Hawaiian system of taboo created a peaceful community based on strict rules.

1. Decide whether these statements are carefully crafted. Circle your answer.

   a. Taboo was a system that treated men better than women without reason.   Yes/No

   b. Taboo was a system used by Hawaiians many years ago.   Yes/No

   c. Under taboo children could not enter the chieftain's tent.   Yes/No

   d. Children were treated unfairly by taboo.   Yes/No

   e. The Hawaiian term for the taboo system is *kapu*.   Yes/No

2. Using the information below, write your own carefully crafted statement about the different islands of Hawaii.

Hawaiian Island	Important fact
Oahu	the most populated island
Big Island	has an active volcano
Molokai	"The Friendly Isle"
Kauai	"The Garden Isle"
Lanai	the smallest inhabited island

Guidance

Writing an article about understanding others' points of view and cultures requires you to:

- make general points about why it is important to show respect
- use details and examples to support your points.

An article of about 200 words requires four general points and an example for each.

3. Here are some suggested general points. Provide a specific example to support each one.

   a. It is interesting to learn about the customs of other cultures.

   ----

   b. Respecting other cultures means your own culture is respected too.

   ----

   c. Other cultures will have important lessons you can learn.

----

   d. Understanding other cultures makes it easier to live together in peace.

----

4. For your own article, decide on your first general point and specific example. Use the space below to write your paragraph.

Writing

5. Using your plans, on a separate sheet of paper write about 200 words to complete the following task:

- Write a carefully crafted article about understanding others' points of view and cultures.

Skills checklist

When you have finished your 200-word carefully crafted article, complete the following checklist.

? Have you created four general points?

? Have you chosen four appropriate examples to support your points?

? Have you considered your choice of words so your points are carefully crafted?

? Have you written in a semi-formal style?

? Have you made every word count?

Checking your progress

1. Edgar H Schein wrote: "Most of my important lessons about life have come from recognising how others from a different culture view things." Write a quote that sums up how you feel about the importance of understanding others' customs and cultures.

Grammar

2. Which will always come first, inference or implication?

----

3. Which two inferences might be the result of the following implication? Tick your answers.

   ● In the taboo system in Hawaii, no one was allowed to enter the chieftain's hut without permission from him.

      a. The chieftain was not very important. ☐

      b. The chieftain was always a man. ☐

      c. The chieftain didn't like visitors. ☐

4. Write down the correct antonym for each of the words below.

   a. decided: _____

   b. forwards: _____

   c. slow: _____

5. Underline the positive words in each of the sentences.

   a. Magnificent scenery, a sparkling ocean and clear blue skies make Hawaii a dream destination.

   b. There was no greater or more honoured king than Kamehameha.

   c. The *koa*, expertly crafted handmade canoes, were strong, quick and unsinkable.

Writing

6. When using more neutral words which of these statements apply? Tick your answers.

   a. Opinions are stronger. ☐   **c.** A more balanced point of view is expressed. ☐

   b. The writing is more measured. ☐   **d.** Implications are still made. ☐

7. What is implied by each of these statements?

a. Only 20 per cent of the population of Hawaii are native to the islands.

----

b. Most Hawaiians live on Oahu in and around the capital, Honolulu.

----

8. Which one of these sentences is carefully crafted? Tick your answer.

a. I believe that every culture has a lesson that can be learned by those outside it.

b. While understanding that a different culture may have some value, it is important to accept that many cultures have failed to survive time.

9. Rewrite the following paragraph using neutral words and no opinions.

The Hawaiian people have one of the most limited languages in the world with only twelve letters in the alphabet. This accounts for the many words with repeated sounds that are so difficult to pronounce and is the reason why a word such as aloha can have three different meanings. No wonder the language is dying.

----

10. Now it is time to make an evaluation of your progress through this chapter. Circle your response.

a. How confident are you when:

• *Using antonyms?*	very	quite	sometimes	not very	I need help
• *Using implication and inference?*	very	quite	sometimes	not very	I need help
• *Using positive, negative or neutral words?*	very	quite	sometimes	not very	I need help

b. Which statement below best describes you? Tick your response.

• *I know that different kinds of words create different tones, but I find it hard to choose.*

• *I recognise how important implication and inference are and use them – although not always successfully.*

• I'm confident that I understand how to use implication and inference to carefully craft my writing.

c. Write a question of your own about how to carefully craft your writing. Have an answer ready and try it out on someone you know.

Imagine you are a city planner. You are attending a conference to discuss your city's future. At this conference you are going to deliver a speech in which you set out your vision of how your city will look in 100 years' time. Which of these alternatives will you choose to support?

huge skyscrapers   **an underground city**   **a sky city floating above the clouds**

I will support _____

because _____

Future dreams

A hundred years ago, sending a man to the moon was **considered** a work of fiction. Fifty years ago, the idea that a computer the size of a wristwatch, with more processing power than any of those used in the moon missions, would be available for consumers to buy seemed **unimaginable**. Today, our language is **littered** with vocabulary connected to technology. Gigabyte, terabyte and Internet are all commonly used terms that children grow-up with. If you ask a 5-year-old child "What is a mouse?" the answer might involve a reference to computing rather than the furry rodent. Such is progress.

Yet are we as advanced as we think we are? In 50 or 100 years' time, what wonders we can only imagine now will be seen as a normal part of daily life? Will we have tamed Mars, built cities below the deepest oceans and think cars have always flown across **virtual** highways in the sky? Will future generations look back at the early 21st century and smile at how **backward** and limited technology was, just as we now view the early 20th century? All progress is the result of those who dare to imagine and to think beyond the **conventional.** Are you ready to dream?

Building your vocabulary

considered:	thought to be
unimaginable:	impossible to think will happen
littered:	full of
virtual:	not physically present
backward:	out of date or old-fashioned
conventional:	accepted as normal

1. According to the passage, what would have been considered impossible 100 years ago?

   ----

2. Which area of technology is littered with the terms *virtual*, *gigabyte* and *terabyte*?

   ----

3. Why is it necessary to invent new words and terms or change the meanings of others to explain new technology? For example, think of *Internet* and *mouse*.

   ----

4. How might future generations consider our technology to be backward and limited?

   ----

5. What do you think will be the biggest advance in technology in the next 50 years?

   ----

6. In your view, why is it important to think beyond the conventional and unimaginable when considering future technology?

Complex past tense

Looking closely

The tense you choose to use depends upon time. There are three basic tenses: *past, present* and *future*. Which one you choose informs the reader when the action is happening. For example:

- **Past:**   Sailing ships were the only way to travel around the world.
- **Present:**   Modern airlines offer a safe way to travel around the world.
- **Future:**   In 2100 tourists will be able to travel into space.

Another basic past tense is the *past continuous*, as shown below:

- What were you doing when the 2014 football World Cup started?

Sometimes a simple past tense is not appropriate and a more complex version is needed. Sometimes you will want to write that an action happened before another one in the past or that it happened before a certain point in time. You use the *past perfect* tense to do this, for example:

- Shayla *visited* the police station because she *lost* her purse in Venice.
- I never *had understood* computers before I *did* the course at college.

1. Put a tick by the sentences written in the past perfect tense.

    a. Roshan passed the science test with top marks because he had studied the night before it took place.

    b. I went to Australia last year.

    c. Lily knew her way around the city because she had been there many times before.

    d. I am visiting the local history museum this morning.

    e. When he went to the theme park yesterday it was special as he had never been to one before.

Looking closely

You can also use the past perfect tense to show *how long* an action had been happening before the event in the past being described. For example:

- When he *left* college to go abroad he *had been* studying *for four years*.
- As she *boarded* the airplane she *realised* she *had been* using the same airline *for over ten years*.

A third way you can use the past perfect tense is to write in general terms how long an action took place before the event being described. For instance:

- The teacher *read* all the essays *before* he *marked* any of them.
- The man *bought* his new computer just *before* the price *dropped* by 20 per cent.

2. Read the sentences and circle the correct options to change them into the past perfect tense.

    a. She (*catch/caught/catching*) the 8.00 a.m. train as she (*had done/is doing/will do*) for the last ten years.

    b. He had never (*saw/seen*) a robot before the exhibition even though he had (*studied/study/studying*) robots for five years.

    c. Dilshan had (*complete/completed*) his third year at university when he (*passes/pass/passed*) his degree.

    d. I (*watch/watched*) all the *Star Wars* movies in a week before I (*go/went/will go*) to the exhibition.

    e. Simone (*feels/is feeling/felt*) lonely for two years before she (*will meet/meets/met*) her new best friend.

3. Change these sentences into the past perfect tense. The first one is done for you.

    a. I will write the article before you give me the details.

        I <u>wrote</u> the article before you <u>gave</u> me the details.

    b. I want to go to the cinema but my friend does not.

        ----

    c. Before we land on the moon many engineers will work on the project.

        ----

    d. Great events happen in the past before records are kept.

        ----

    e. Many businessmen see the advantages of the Internet long before it first appears.

Teacher tip

The more complex forms of the past tense you can use, the better your language will appear to others. Check out the *past perfect continuous* as your next step on the way to recognising different past tenses, how they work and when to use them.

Determiners and demonstrative pronouns

Remember

Determiners are words that are placed directly before a noun or noun phrase and determine their state. The most common determiners are *the*, *a* and *an*, but there are many more that show possession, how much and how many. Some words act as both demonstrative pronouns and determiners.

Looking closely

The word *the* is called the definite article. It is placed before the noun or noun phrase to show that the people or things being referred to are specific, such as:

- *The* future is unknown but *the* past is recorded.

In this example there is only one future and one past being referred to, so *the* is used to show this is specific.

The words *a* and *an* are the indefinite article. When the noun begins with a vowel *an* is used and if it begins with a consonant *a* is used. The indefinite article is used to refer to nouns in general non-specific terms. It is only used when the noun is singular. For example:

- *An* early part of history was referred to as the dinosaur age.

- *A* dinosaur could be a carnivore, herbivore or omnivore.

1. Write a sentence of between 12 and 20 words using these nouns (the noun phrase in **c**) with their definite article.

   a. caveman: _____

   b. president: _____

   c. gold medallist: _____

2. Circle the correct indefinite article for each of the following sentences.

   a. Without doubt (*a/an*) injured dinosaur wouldn't last long.

   b. I would love to study (*a/an*) herd of dinosaurs.

   c. How would (*a/an*) peaceful dinosaur protect itself from (*a/an*) predator?

Looking closely

This, *that*, *these* and *those* are also determiners when placed before a noun, for example:

- *This* century is only just beginning,

- How many of *these* books are about history?

My, *your*, *his*, *her*, *its*, *our* and *their* show possession when used with a noun. For instance:

- On meeting *my* ancestors, I would ask for *their* views on life.

- Do you believe *his* idea or mine? Whichever you choose, you need to justify *your* decision.

3. Underline the determiners in this paragraph.

> My friend Onkay is very interested in her history. She is fascinated by those moments when her family made life-changing decisions. These choices shaped who she is today and remind her of that period in time when life was very hard. Her friend James also likes his history, but its charm is in all the battles fought by his ancestors. Our opinions are very different, but I can see their point about history being important. That idea we all agree on.

Looking closely

Some determiners can also be used as demonstrative pronouns, but these do not have to be placed directly before a noun. In fact, a demonstrative pronoun can be used in place of the noun, such as:

- **Without demonstrative pronoun:** The first *Star Wars* movie was so exciting. The first *Star Wars* movie is my favourite.

- **Using demonstrative pronoun:** The first *Star Wars* movie was extremely exciting. *That* is my favourite.

Two other demonstrative pronouns are: *none* and *neither*

Both *neither* and *none* are negatives and are plural as *neither* applies to two and *none* to more than two.

4. There are four common demonstrative pronouns, two are singular and two plural. Use one to complete each sentence below.

Singular:		**Plural:**	
this	that	these	those

a. In the future cities will be built on Mars; --------------- will be below the surface.

b. Each family will live in its own apartment. --------------- will contain everything the family needs.

c. Living underground is necessary because the atmosphere is poisonous so --------------- who don't like being inside all the time will find it difficult.

d. Not being able to go outside; --------------- will be the hardest part.

5. Complete this passage with the correct demonstrative pronoun.

> People will be transported to Mars in huge spaceships. As it will be a one-way trip, --------------- will return to Earth. Both the journey and settling in a new home on a new planet will not be easy. --------------- should be taken lightly.

Teacher tip

Determiners are also used to show how many or how much. *All, any, some, each* and *every* are just some examples of these. Numerals such as *one, two, first* and *second* are also determiners when placed before a noun. Do some research to build up your own collection of determiners to use in your writing.

The apostrophe and speech marks

Remember

The apostrophe has two main uses:

1. It is used to show the shortened form of two words when one or more letters have been left out. When this happens the new word becomes a contraction.

2. The apostrophe is used to show that an object belongs to someone or something else. This is called possession.

Looking closely

When writing or speaking in a semi-formal or informal situation you can shorten the words you use by putting two together. For example, when writing a formal essay you would write:

- I *would not* be able to live without my mobile phone!

When writing to a friend you might write:

- I *wouldn't* be able to live without my mobile phone!

1. Here are some other commonly used contractions. Draw lines to match the formal version to the shortened one. One is done for you.

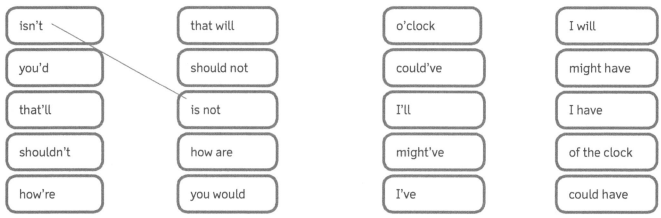

Looking closely

Most contractions follow the same rule with the apostrophe being placed where the missing letter or letters would have been, such as:

- *should have* becomes *should've* with the apostrophe where the *ha* was.

However, some contractions are irregular and the apostrophe is harder to place, such as:

- *shall not* becomes *shan't because* even though both the *ll* and *o* are missing only one apostrophe is used.

Be careful when using *I'd* as it can mean *I would* or *I had* and can cause confusion.

Contractions when *is* comes after a noun can also be confusing, for example:

- **Singular:** *The <u>future is</u> in front of us* becomes *the <u>future's</u> in front of us* – use an apostrophe

- **Plural:** Our <u>futures</u> are ahead of us both – no apostrophe because there are two <u>futures</u>.

2. Cross out the incorrect word or words to create a correct sentence for each of the following.

    a. (*Times/Time's*) on our side for once.

    b. How many (*times/time's*) do I have to tell you the future is bright?

    c. (*Whose/Who's*) interested in space travel?

    d. Remember to book our (*flights/flight's*) for our week at the space hotel.

Looking closely

When you want to show that something belongs to someone or something else use an apostrophe.

- **Singular:** *The <u>suit of the astronaut</u> protected him* becomes *the <u>astronaut's suit</u> protected him.*
- **Plural:** *The <u>suits of the two astronauts</u> protected them* becomes *the two <u>astronauts' suits</u> protected them.*

---

3. Complete these sentences correctly.

    a. The _____ (spaceship) engines were not working so it was drifting in space.

    b. The _____ (planet) atmosphere was full of dangerous gas.

    c. The planet had two moons. The _____ (moon) surfaces were lifeless.

    d. The _____ (captain) meeting showed they were concerned about the fleet.

    e. The _____ (ship) captain was in complete control of the situation.

Looking closely

Speech marks are used to show direct speech, such as:

- "Where will I be in five years' time" asked Samantha.

You do not use speech marks to show reported speech, such as:

- I heard Samantha ask where she will be in five years' time.

---

4. Decide which of these sentences need speech marks and add them.

    a. Sara's teacher asked, Sara, do you think cars will fly in the future?

    b. I'm not sure but I hope so because a flying car would be really cool, replied Sara.

    c. Her friend Lily was not so sure and said that flying a car would be dangerous.

    d. Sara laughed and said, come on Lily, it would be such fun to drive a flying car.

    e. Their teacher also laughed saying he wouldn't want to be anywhere near her when Sara started driving.

Writing a balanced article

Some people would like to live in the past rather than the future. What do you think?

- The past is better because life was more simple then.

- I love technology and can't wait for all the new inventions in the future.

- I'm looking forward to the future, but progress isn't only about new technology.

I would like to live in the _____

because _____

You are going to write a balanced article about the pros and cons of progress.

Guidance

An article is a piece of writing on a specific subject; in this case progress and whether it is good or bad. Articles appear in newspapers, magazines and on the Internet. A balanced article will look at both sides and treat them equally, without choosing which is best.

1. The pros are the good points and the cons are the bad points.

   a. Draw lines to match these pros and cons. One is done for you.

Pros		Cons
People will live longer		Carbon dioxide levels will increase
Computers will be more powerful	**BUT**	The world's population will increase
Robots will do lots of manual jobs		No countryside will be left
Travel will be easier		We will rely on computers too much
Everyone will live in modern cities		People will be unemployed

   b. Now write three of your own pros and cons regarding how technology will affect our lives in the future.

   BUT

   BUT

   BUT

   ----

2. A balanced article will explain both the pros and cons of the ideas being discussed without choosing one particular side. Decide whether these statements are balanced or not. Tick those that are balanced and put a cross next to those that aren't.

    a. Without question an increase in world population will lead to terrible problems.

    b. In the future there may be a big increase in the world's population which may lead to a shortage of food, but farming techniques may well improve so much that all the food we need will be provided.

    c. Robots will make our lives much better because they'll do all the boring jobs.

    d. Robots may become more useful by doing many tasks, but will this have an effect on the rate of unemployment in countries?

Phrasal verbs are word phrases that are used in semi-formal, informal writing and speech. They have a more general meaning than the more specific verb they've replaced. They are useful if you don't know the specific verb.

Here are some examples:

- Instead of *sustain* use *keep going* – Underwater cities are expensive to *keep going*.

- Instead of *maintain* use *look after* – It takes many people to *look after* a complicated spaceship.

3. Work out which phrasal verbs to use in these sentences. The first one is done for you.

put it together	turn down	break down	sort out	wake up

    a. When you <u>break down</u> (divide) the number of hours you spend on building a robot servant is it value for money?

    b. Your robot servant should be ready when you _____ (awake) in the morning.

    c. Your robot servant should never _____ (refuse) a reasonable request.

    d. Every day you need to _____ (organise) your robot's list of jobs.

    e. When you first buy your robot you have to _____ (assemble) yourself.

4. Match the phrasal verb to the specific verb.

add up to	support
back up	equal
figure out	discover
find out	enter
go in	indicate
look into	understand
point out	investigate

Your balanced article

Planning

There are three different writing styles you can use to write your balanced article: formal, semi-formal or informal. Which one you use depends on the audience for your piece of writing.

You are going to write your article in a semi-formal writing style, so consider the following:

- Write in the first or third person and address the reader directly using the second person.

- You may use contractions and abbreviations.

- You may use phrasal verbs, for example *thought about* instead of *pondered* or *get up* instead of *arise*.

- You may use idioms, though not too many, but not slang or text language.

- Correct punctuation and grammar are still important.

1. Change each of the formal sentences below into a semi-formal one. The first is completed as an example.

    a. In the future robots will complete all the perfunctory tasks within the household, but cannot be expected to exhibit higher-order thinking skills.

    In the future robots will do all the little jobs in the home, but don't expect them to think for themselves.

    b. Robots do not have personalities and will not behave as humans would.

    ----

    c. When purchasing a robot house servant several factors have to be considered.

    ----

    d. Programming a robot is the responsibility of the owner.

    ----

2. In a balanced article you will write about the pros and cons, but first you must decide what the key ideas are. Place the ideas below in your order of importance, by writing 1 for the most important and 5 for the least important.

    a. More advanced technology

    b. More space exploration

    c. Cities in the oceans

    d. Better medicines to stop diseases

    e. People will have more leisure time

Add two of your own ideas to the list.

f. ---
    ----

g. ---

Guidance

It is important to develop your key ideas. Say, for example, that one of your key ideas is *cities under the ocean*. You need to develop it by writing about the pros and cons. For instance:

- **Pros:** The cities will give people a different lifestyle away from crowded cities on land.
- **Cons:** The underwater cities will be expensive to build and sustain and will be difficult to reach.

3. Which of the following is the best-developed and balanced response to this idea? Tick your answer.

    a. These underwater cities will be amazing. The people who live there will be able to swim with whales and see dolphins every day. They will live in a perfect world with no crime and plenty of space.

    b. Such cities will take too long to build and be too expensive to run.

    c. Underwater cities may well be wonderful places to live and offer a special experience, but the difficulties in building them and the huge cost of maintaining them must be taken into account when deciding if they should be created.

Writing

4. Using your plans, on a separate sheet of paper write a balanced article of 150—200 words on the following question:

- What are the pros and cons of progress?

Skills checklist

When you have finished your balanced article, complete the following checklist.

? Have you made a plan using key ideas?

? Have you covered both sides of each idea so your response is balanced?

? Have you developed your key ideas?

? Have you written in a semi-formal style?

? Have you made every word count?

Checking your progress

1. Deepak Chopra wrote: "When you make a choice, you change the future." Write a quote that sums up how you feel about the future.

Grammar

2. Explain why the following sentence is an example of the past perfect tense.

   • I had never liked history before I visited the museum.

   ----

3. Underline the two definite articles used in the sentence below.

   • How we view the future depends on the trust we have in technology.

4. Choose the correct indefinite articles in this passage. Circle your answers.

   I am not (a/an) scientist or (a/an) engineer but I am (a/an) fan of technology. Give me (a/an) new piece of technology and I am (a/an) child in (a/an) toy shop. I will play with it for (a/an) long time and never be bored. What (a/an) amazing thing the future will be if we give it (a/an) chance!

5. Add an apostrophe in the correct place in each sentence below.

   a. The past isnt a place I would like to live.

   b. You dont have to be a historian to love the past.

   c. Its corridors filled with laughing children, the old museums atmosphere was alive again.

   d. The two pupils faces were filled with wonder at the dinosaur skeleton.

   e. I shant look at another history book ever again!

Writing

6. Underline the phrasal verbs in these sentences.

   a. When you buy a robot servant you should shop around for the best price.

   b. When you train a robot servant you have to put up with the time it takes.

   c. You need to be consistent in your training so keep doing the same thing over and over.

7. Write a con relating to each of these pros about progress.

   a. The oceans will be full of huge super ships each a mile in length but

   ----

   b. People will no longer have to work long hours in boring jobs but

   ----

   c. Children will grow up in cities on the Moon and Mars but

   ----

8. Which of these is the most balanced point? Tick your answer.

   a. The future will be a terrible place to live.

   b. I'm excited by the future because there will be lots of new inventions, but I'm also scared by the thought of robots taking over the world.

   c. Scientists predict that it will be possible for humans to travel to other planets and build communities, but it remains to be seen if the cost of such missions will be too high.

9. Develop this balanced idea to make a strong point.

- While there will be many who find the idea of travelling through space exciting, scientists believe the journeys will be dangerous with no guarantee of success.

----

10. Now it is time to make an evaluation of your progress through this chapter. Circle your response.

   a. How confident are you when:

Using the past perfect tense?	very	quite	sometimes	not very	I need help
Using demonstrative pronouns?	very	quite	sometimes	not very	I need help
Using apostrophes and speech marks?	very	quite	sometimes	not very	I need help

   b. Which statement best describes you? Tick your response.

- I know what an article is, but find it hard to write with balance.

- I recognise different viewpoints create balance, but it is hard for me to write a balanced article in my own words.

- I'm confident that I understand how to write an article that is balanced.

   c. Write a question of your own about how to write a balanced article. Have an answer ready and try it out on someone you know.

Communication

Read the information below and circle the facts you know. Underline other details you think are facts.

- Lysander was a Greek army general who led the army in the town of Sparta. He died in 395BC.

- Julius Caesar was a famous Roman Emperor, in charge of the Roman Empire. He was born in 100BC and lived until 44BC, when he was stabbed by several of his senators in the senate in Rome.

- Mary was Queen of Scotland from 1542 until 1567. She wanted to rule England as well but Elizabeth I, her cousin, ruled from 1558 until 1603.

Codes in history

In 405BC the Greek general Lysander of Sparta was sent a coded message written on the inside of a servant's belt. When Lysander wound the belt around a wooden **baton** the message was revealed. The message warned Lysander that Persia was about to go to war against him. He immediately **set sail** and defeated the Persians. ...

The Roman ruler Julius Caesar (100BC - 44BC) used a very simple **cipher** for secret communication. He **substituted** each letter of the alphabet with a letter three positions along, so that **A** became **D**, **B** became **E** and so on. His famous phrase **VENI, VIDI, VICI** ("I came, I saw, I conquered") would have read **YHQL YLGL YLFL**.... After **the fall** of the Roman Empire codes were not used much until the sixteenth century. ...

In Elizabethan England Mary Queen of Scots sent coded messages to her supporters who were plotting to murder Queen Elizabeth I. The messages were **intercepted** by the head of Elizabeth's secret service, Sir Francis Walsingham. He **deciphered** them and discovered the plot. ...

Source: http://www.macs.hw.ac.uk/~foss/valentin/Codes&Cyphers.html

Building your vocabulary

baton: smooth thin stick

set sail: begin a journey by ship

cipher: a code, secret writing

substituted: replaced

the fall: capture or defeat

intercepted: stopped from reaching the intended destination

deciphered: broke the code

1. In which country was one of the earliest codes used?

----

2. How did Lysander read the codes he was sent?

----

3. Who would you name a code after and why?

----

4. In your view, which method of hiding a message is the best and why?

----

5. In your view, why might a code cause a problem rather than help? What might happen?

----

6. How would you create your own code? How would you send it?

Formal and informal vocabulary

Remember

Formal vocabulary is used in formal settings, for example when writing a letter to apply for a job or when talking to someone important. Informal vocabulary is used when writing an informal letter to a friend, for example, or when chatting to friends in a relaxed setting.

1. Decide whether each of these forms of communication is formal. Write the letter **F** or **I** in the box beside each word. Then add a formal alternative for each informal word, and an informal alternative for each formal word.

   Phone ☐ _____

   Note ☐ _____

   Conversation ☐ _____

   Meeting ☐ _____

2. Read the two messages below.

A	B
Hi Pete	Dear Mr Green
Coming home soon – can't wait to see you all again. Please pick me up as I have loads of bags with me.	I am returning soon and am looking forward to meeting you again. Please arrange a car to collect me as I will be travelling with several items of luggage.
Thanks	Yours sincerely
Don	Don Brown

   a. Which message is formal?

   _____

   b. How do you know the message is formal? List two things that tell you.

   _____

   _____

Looking closely

You decide what vocabulary to use in a piece of writing depending on whether the writing is formal or informal, and that will depend on whom you are writing to. If you are writing to a long-standing friend, you will use informal words; if you are writing to someone you do not know or only slightly know, then you will use more formal vocabulary. Choosing the right vocabulary for your writing will have a significant impact on the overall success of the piece. The wrong word or phrase will have a negative effect as it will break the flow of the writing.

3. Rewrite this short letter changing the underlined words into more formal words or phrases.

Dear Mal,

I'm writing to <u>ask for a favour</u> as I have a project for school and I need to <u>learn about</u> computers and how they have changed the way we <u>talk to each other</u>. I know you <u>are into that sort of thing</u>, so can I <u>come over some time</u>? <u>Let me know as soon as possible</u>.

Love,

Lola

Language to achieve conciseness

Remember

When you write, you have a purpose, which is to tell the target reader something. The best way to do this is as concisely as possible because this speeds up the whole process while maintaining the interest of the target reader.

1. Tick the sentences you think are concise.

   a. See me at 7.30 p.m. under the clock at Waterloo.

   b. I think it would be a good idea if we met near the gatehouse of the blue garden, which is prettier than the red one, don't you think?

   c. It will start at 2 p.m. so don't be late.

   d. In my opinion, I think that one of the best ways to communicate is to have a conversation face to face with people rather than sending a message they might not even receive.

2. Draw lines to match a sentence on the left with its more concise version on the right.

   a. I am writing about a new code and the new code has just been cracked by codebreaker Juan Roig.

   b. I would like to listen to Jacob Ng because when he talks he is always very interesting.

   c. Henry always wanted to learn physics so he would have the knowledge to invent the perfect communications system.

   i Jacob Ng is always very interesting to listen to.

   ii Henry studied physics to invent the ultimate communications system.

   iii I am writing about Juan Roig and the code he cracked.

Teacher tip

You can achieve conciseness in both formal and informal writing. Sometimes you have to write a set number of words (for example in an essay) but you must also ensure you use each word carefully and are not just writing an extra sentence to reach the word limit. Make sure your sentences add substance, not just padding.

3. Put the following text into the correct order to make one concise paragraph. Write out the paragraph on the lines below.

- He thinks it is similar to translating from one language to another
- Raz has always been interested in other languages
- but unfortunately the hardest part for him is not knowing the language the code has been written in.
- he first heard about them.
- but his favourite hobby is cracking codes.
- he has thought that being able to crack codes has helped his own language learning.
- He has always found them fun to do and
- Raz has cracked codes ever since

Remember

Always plan and proofread your writing, so the final work delivers a concise idea with appropriate vocabulary and maintains the interest of the reader; combining short sentences or using a subordinate clause can help you do this.

Using tenses for shades of meaning

1. The verb tenses we use can change the whole meaning of a sentence where the rest of the sentence remains unchanged. Look at these pairs of sentences and focus on the tenses in each sentence. Then explain the difference in meaning between the two sentences.

   a. I sent my mother a coded message.

   b. I had sent my mother a coded message.

   ----

   c. I had worked in Shanghai when I made the call.

   d. I was working in Shanghai when I made the call.

Looking closely

You have to consider a past effect on the present or a present condition that contrasts with the past. This includes skills you have learned that you still have today, even if you do not use them or improve them on a regular basis. For example, if you had piano lessons in the past, you can still play the piano today. Take the sentence below:

- I had piano lessons as a child.

Although the piano lessons were in the past, they have an effect on the present because you are still able to play, even if you no longer have piano lessons.

2. Think of five events in the past that have a present effect.

For example:

- I went to football practice every week.
- Present effect – I know how to play football.

a. _____

_____

b. _____

_____

c. _____

_____

d. _____

_____

e. _____

_____

3. Add the correct tenses below to complete this dialogue between two friends talking about past events and present effect.

Paula: I _____ to Paris this summer. I am looking forward to it.

Sophia: You must go to the Louvre. It _____ a wonderful museum.

Paula: _____ you _____ to the Louvre?

Sophia: Yes, I _____ to Paris when I was 12. I learned some French when I was there.

Paula: Did you learn to speak fluently?

Sophia: Not when I _____ there but I came back and had lessons for several years.

4. Use the verbs in brackets. Put them into an appropriate tense to complete the paragraph.

I _____ (walk) to school last week when I _____ (see)

something amazing. In the field near to where I _____ (live), a big pink circus tent

_____ (appear) overnight. It _____ (be) huge and

_____ (look) very exciting.

Teacher tip

Changing nothing but the tense of a verb in a sentence can dramatically alter the overall meaning of the sentence, so you need to make sure you have chosen the right one for the meaning you wish to give.

Formal register
Guidance

Register is the type of writing you use according to the purpose you have for writing or speaking. For example, you will have to use a formal register to write to your boss or to apply for a job. However, you will use an informal register when you write to friends or in your diary.

1. When was the last time you used a formal register? Write a sentence explaining what you wrote about and why you decided it had to be in a formal register.

    ---

2. You use a formal register in several different types of writing. Add four more examples to the list started below.

    a. Letter to apply for a job

    b. ---

    c. ---

    d. ---

    e. ---

3. Formal register requires words and phrases to be written in full. Identify the contractions and write them out in full.

    a. It isn't there. ---

    b. We'll meet you at 6. ---

    c. They don't use Morse code anymore. ---

    d. I've seen an advert for a code maker. ---

4. Read the five opinions taken from formal writing and choose from the box the type of writing each one comes from.

    > report   work email   letter of complaint
    > application letter   letter to your boss

    a. I would recommend we implement this system as soon as we can in order to protect our databases.

        ---

    b. I am very grateful to you for considering my position.

        ---

    c. I would be grateful if you could finish it today and send it to me via email.

        ---

d. I hope to hear from you in the near future.

----

e. I feel I would be an asset to your department.

----

5. Explain which words in each opinion helped you match it to the correct type of writing.

----

6. Combine the phrases below to make two sentences of formal writing. Remember to change the punctuation.

- invented by the Romans and
- named after Julius Caesar who is well known as a Roman Emperor
- The Romans wanted to find out what their enemies were saying
- so they could decide what action to take in order to defeat them
- one of the earliest codes was

a. ---

----

b. ---

Teacher tip

Before you start to write, make a note of the register you plan to use. When you are proofreading, look at the vocabulary and the sentence structures you have used and check they are appropriate for the register you intended to use.

Writng a formal report

1. Here are some phrases you would see in writing, but which ones would appear in a report? Tick the correct phrases.

   a. The new shop has been welcomed ☐

   b. See you soon ☐

   c. Dear Fiona ☐

   d. I look forward to hearing from you soon ☐

   e. City Centre ☐

   f. Yours sincerely ☐

Planning

2. You are going to write a formal report on codebreaking. Choosing the right vocabulary for your report is important if you want to create a positive effect on the target reader. Choose three words or phrases you will use in your report.

   a. Secure communication: messages sent and received safely without others reading them ☐

   b. Substitution: changing one letter or number for another ☐

   c. Binary alphabet: changing letters into a sequence of numbers using only 0 and 1 ☐

   d. Battle tactics: plans for attacking or retreating from an enemy ☐

   e. Frequency analysis: working out how often a letter or number appears (in a code) ☐

   f. Invincible: unbreakable ☐

Guidance

When you write a report, organise your ideas under subheadings so one heading summarises one key idea. It adds clarity for the reader. Add no more than one explanation or reason per idea; this allows you to persuade the reader without being overtly persuasive.

A formal report needs formal register and vocabulary. You need to include facts based on figures or independent opinion (a survey, for example). You can end the report with a recommendation, but for the rest of the report do not include your opinions.

3. Here are some facts about codebreaking you can include in your report. Add two facts from the list below to each heading.

Historic codes	**Codebreaking today**	**Codes in the future**
_____	_____	_____
_____	_____	_____

- Mostly done on computers
- Done entirely by robots
- Used ribbons and wood to hide codes
- One method named after a Roman emperor
- Some might even be unbreakable
- Sometimes using methods that have been used for centuries

Writing

4. You have recently been learning about codes. Write a report giving information about the most interesting details you have learned and what codes have been and can be used for. Write about 150 words.

Skills checklist

When you have finished your report, complete the following checklist.

? Have you included information about codes? ☐

? Have you used three separate ideas? ☐

? Have you used a formal register? ☐

? Have you used headings for the main paragraphs? ☐

? Have you included your opinions? ☐

? Have you written a concise report? ☐

Checking your progress

1. The Nobel Prize-winning playwright, George Bernard Shaw, said "The single biggest problem in communication is the illusion that it has taken place." Write your own quote about communication.

Grammar

2. Tick the two sentences below that use formal vocabulary.

   a. The codebreaking club was brill – you'd have loved it.

   b. He'd used a formal register this time.

   c. It was a remarkable display of communication skills.

   d. He had to remember to use an informal register in his letter.

3. Rewrite the following two sentences into one more concise sentence.

   When the codebreakers saw what they had to do, they decided that the best way was to use the frequency method. The frequency method works very well with longer texts and the one they had to crack was a longer text.

----

4. Explain the difference in meaning between the two sentences below.
   - I called Tony when I read the message.
   - I called Tony when I was reading the message.

----

5. Tick the sentence below that has been written in a formal register.

   a. It was five o'clock and we were really excited about getting the latest message from him.

   b. At 1700 we received the message that we would have to wait ten minutes before starting the race.

Writing

6. You have been asked to write a report on communication. Give three headings you would use in this report.

a. --

b. --

c. --

7. Write four words or phrases using a formal register that would help you write an interesting report about communication.

----

8. If you were writing a report on effective forms of communication, which one would you recommend as the best? Write one sentence to give your recommendation.

----

9. a. Write one sentence to explain the effect using a formal register has on the reader.

----

b. Write one sentence about how people communicate using formal register. Then write another sentence to explain why it is formal.

----

10 a. Which statement best describes you? Tick your response.

- I know what a report is, but struggle to use concise and formal language.

- I understand how to organise my ideas concisely and formally, but find it hard to incorporate these skills in my reports.

- I'm confident that I understand how to organise my ideas into paragraphs and can use my skills to write concise and formal reports.

b. Write a question of your own for a partner. You will ask your partner which areas in this chapter he or she has improved the most. Use the following features in your question.

- formal vocabulary
- concise writing
- shades of meaning in tenses
- formal register
- writing a report

----

12 Global issues

Which global issues are important in your community? Add two examples to the list below:

- global warming
- pollution from cars and other vehicles
- too much rubbish
- too much food waste

Japan's Kamikatsu: The first zero waste town?

In 2003, the Japanese town of Kamikatsu declared its Zero Waste Ambition. Since then the residents of Kamikatsu have adopted arguably the most **rigorous** recycling programme in the world. In 2016 this rural community is well under way to **eliminating** 100 per cent of its waste.

...Once the townspeople burned rubbish outside or dumped it on farms – something that was never a problem when all of the waste was **organic**.

As trends in **consumption** moved towards more packaged goods and **non biodegradable** plastics the old system would no longer work. Burning the items also began to raise health concerns due to the release of powerful toxins.

It was then that the focus turned on recycling and the 'Zero waste' initiative was put into motion, a movement focused on creating a **sustainable** lifestyle, with no need for incineration or landfill. The town started with nine categories of waste separation; by 2002 the number of categories grew to 34.

Today you will find no rubbish trucks in Kamikatsu. People take their waste to a town collection centre and separate it into the various categories themselves. Each space or box is labelled to show where it will be recycled, what it will become and how much it will cost.

Source: http://www.wearesalt.org/japans-kamikatsu-the-first-zero-waste-town/

Building your vocabulary

rigorous: strict

eliminating: getting rid of

organic: natural, not man-made

consumption: use of

non biodegradable: not able to break down completely into the earth

sustainable: able to be maintained

1. When did Kamikatsu first decide it wanted to become a zero waste village?

    ----

2. What made the population of Kamikatsu want zero waste?

    ----

3. Why is burning waste a problem?

    ----

4. Give two of your own adjectives to describe what you think of the zero waste project in Kamikatsu.

    ----

5. How would you feel living in a community with zero waste?

    ----

6. How would you encourage your community to follow the example of Kamikatsu and have zero waste?

Types of sentence

Looking closely

There is more than one type of sentence. Sentences are grouped into categories depending on their purpose. One type of sentence is known as a statement of a fact. These sentences give information, either factual or made up. For example:

- Our community needs to recycle more of the waste it produces.
- The town has built a new play area made from recycled material.
- The factory will now be powered using energy from waste material.

1. Write a statement about recycling in your community.

Looking closely

A question is another type of sentence. There are questions that are used to find out information, so for these a definite answer is required. For example:

- When was the last time you recycled something?

A rhetorical question looks just like any question, but it is question for which no response is required because the answer is implied within it. (Look back to the earlier exercises as a reminder: Chapter 4, page 54.) A rhetorical question might be one that has an obvious answer, but the question is being asked to make a point. For example:

- Should you be recycling more than you already are?
- Are we going to leave all that rubbish on the classroom floor?

2. Write a question about recycling that you would like to ask your local town leaders.

----

3. Write a rhetorical question from your teacher to your class about paper waste.

Looking closely

If you wanted something to be done then you would probably write a sentence known as a command. A command issues an action that needs to be completed or followed. Usually a command is given by someone senior or in charge, such as a teacher or parent. For example, a parent might say:

- "Go and pick up that litter now."

While a command can be expressed strongly, there is another type of sentence called an exclamation that can be used to express strong feeling. Exclamations tend to end with an exclamation mark and are found usually in informal writing. You should use them sparingly. Here is an example:

- There is a village with zero waste – that is amazing!

4. Write a command to your partner about not littering.

5. Write an exclamation about what your partner has done to keep waste down.

6. Think of something you want your classmates to do that they do not do at present. Write it here:

I want my classmates to

7. Choose two sentence types that you could use to ask your partner to do something. Then write two sentences, using the sentence types of your choice.

| statement | question | rhetorical question | command | exclamation |

a.

b.

Remember

A question will expect an answer while a rhetorical question implies the answer in itself. Asking a rhetorical question can be an interesting way to start an article, to engage the reader, but these questions should not be over-used, so try to limit them to one per article.

Relative clauses

Remember

Relative clauses introduce additional information or explanation into a sentence. You can use them to draw the reader into your writing with the additional detail. Relative clauses need a relative pronoun at the start of the clause, a verb and the subject of the clause. For example:

- The man <u>who is wearing the red jumper</u> used to teach my brother about the environment.

In this sentence *who* is the relative pronoun at the start of the relative clause *who is wearing the red jumper*.

1. In the sentences below, underline the relative clause.

   a. The architect who drew the plans for the new houses in the town came to visit the building site today.

   b. The equipment which is needed to cut down the trees is in the barn.

   c. The committee which decided to do a litter pick will come down to the sports field on Tuesday.

   d. The new wind turbine has been built, which is good news.

   e. The companies providing different public services where we live work well together.

Looking closely

Relative clauses will begin with a relative pronoun and you need to make sure you have chosen the correct one for your clause. You should use: *who* if you are talking about a person; *whose* if you are talking about something belonging to or coming from a person; *which* or *that* to refer to an object (moving or inanimate); *where* to refer to a location of something or someone; and *why* when giving a reason. For more examples and explanation, see Chapter 6, page 78.

Here are further examples:

- The man *who* mended the local wind turbine is my cousin.

- The boy *whose* shoes are on the field is in my class.

- The solar panels *that* are on my neighbour's roof are very expensive.

- The country *where* I was born is far from here.

- The reason *why* we had to complete the recycling awareness course was because it would help us think about the planet in the future.

2. Draw lines to match the noun (in the left column) with the relative pronoun that is used with it.

a. The pencil	i. who
b. The city	ii. which/that
c. The teacher	iii. why
d. The reason	iv. where

3. Add the correct relative pronoun to the following sentences.

   a. The small recycling plant _ _ _ _ _ _ _ _ _ _ _ _ _ _ _ _ _ _ is in our town will be expanding next year.

   b. The zoo keeper _ _ _ _ _ _ _ _ _ _ _ _ _ _ _ _ recycles the old bamboo is a very nice lady.

   c. The energy company _ _ _ _ _ _ _ _ _ _ _ _ _ _ _ _ tariffs keep going up is coming under a lot of pressure.

   d. The builders are digging up a piece of land _ _ _ _ _ _ _ _ _ _ _ _ _ _ _ _ a rare butterfly lives.

   e. I wonder if we will move to Mars, _ _ _ _ _ _ _ _ _ _ _ _ _ _ _ is also known as the red planet, as our planet warms up because of global warming.

Looking closely

Some relative clauses are needed for the sentence to make sense and therefore cannot be omitted.

For example:

- The man who is in charge of the power plant works very hard.

Without the relative clause, we do not know which man is being talked about. This is a *defining relative clause*. Here is another example:

- The teacher who is in Classroom 1A teaches us about energy.

If the clause is not necessary for the sentence to make sense, then it is a *non-defining clause*. For example:

- The manager, who I have known for a long time, works very hard.

You do not need to know how long the speaker has known the manager for the sentence to make sense. Here are two more examples:

- Dubai, where my teacher went on holiday, is an interesting place to visit.
- The piano, which I bought last year, would have been used as firewood if I hadn't taken it to be reused.

Note that a non-defining relative clause starts and ends with a comma, whereas there are no commas around a defining clause.

---

4. Add a defining relative clause into each sentence so that it is clear which noun is being talked about.

   a. The bookseller who _ _ _ _ _ _ _ _ _ _ _ _ _ _ _ _ lives next door to my grandparents.

   b. The ball which _ _ _ _ _ _ _ _ _ _ _ _ _ _ _ _ belongs to my neighbour.

   c. The field where _ _ _ _ _ _ _ _ _ _ _ _ _ _ _ _ is now full of flowers.

5. Add a non-defining relative clause to complete each sentence with some extra information.

   a. My local community, _ _ _ _ _ _ _ _ _ _ _ _ _ _ _ _, has built a factory using renewable energy.

   b. The lady, who _ _ _ _ _ _ _ _ _ _ _ _ _ _ _ _, usually recycles everything she buys.

   c. This large town, where _ _ _ _ _ _ _ _ _ _ _ _ _ _ _ _, was built about 20 years ago.

6. Which sentence below contains a defining clause? Tick your answer.

   a. The technology graduate, who has been working at the company for two years, will become famous one day. ☐

   b. The technology graduate who has been taught by Bill Gates will become famous one day. ☐

Figurative meaning

Looking closely

Figurative meaning does not paint a literal picture of what is being described, but uses an analogy to show what is being described.

For example, if you are on your way to the recycling bank with some newspapers and they are feeling heavy, you might say to your friend, "These newspapers weigh a ton." They don't way a ton (about a thousand kilos) and both you and your friend know this, but you both also know that what is meant is that the newspapers are heavy.

For figurative language to work, there has to be mutual understanding of its meaning. Here are two more examples:

- He ordered a cup of coffee and the cup that came was as big as a swimming pool.

The writer knows it wasn't actually the size of even a small pool but is trying to convey that the cup was larger than an average cup.

- I think my homework is going to take years to complete.

The homework might take a bit longer than normal, but homework can often be done in an evening or at most a week, it never takes several years.

1. Draw lines to match the sentences containing a figurative phrase with one of the sentences with the same meaning, but without any figurative meaning.

a. I had to walk miles to the rubbish tip today.	**i.** We used to use twenty trucks to take the rubbish away, but now we only need four.
b. We have got a mountain to climb if we are going to get this finished by 5 p.m.	**ii.** I had to walk nearly a mile to the rubbish tip today.
c. The rubbish used to need millions of trucks to take it away but now it only needs a few.	**iii.** We are going to have to work very hard to get this work finished by 5 p.m.

2. Look at the following comments, which were made on the way to the Kamikatsu recycling plant. What does each speaker actually mean? Write your answers under each speech bubble.

a. "Kamikatsu was drowning in waste until this recycling plant was set up."

----

b. "There were mountains of waste and yet soon there will be none."

----

c. "Members of the town council did not have to wrestle with having to do something – they knew they had to make changes."

----

d. "I heard that the Kamikatsu zero waste plan will be smelling success by 2020."

Remember

Like rhetorical questions, figurative meaning can spark the reader's interest in what you are saying, but you need to use it in moderation. If you include a lot of figurative meaning, it could distract the reader from the main points you are making.

Writing a blog

Looking closely

A *blog* is an informal piece of writing which has been uploaded onto the Internet for people to read. It might be a chosen group who have been asked to read the blog or it might be that the blog has been made available for anyone to read.

A blog uses informal language to describe and discuss issues which mean something to the writer. The writer of a blog is also called a *blogger*.

Blogs can be used to react to events which have happened, even on the day they have happened. The individual entries on a blog are called *posts* and bloggers often upload a post each day, so the whole blog acts like an online diary of their thoughts and feelings.

1. If you had a blog, what would you write about? Write one sentence and then explain your choice.

Remember

You have probably read or written a blog that has been posted online. Before bloggers post their blogs online, they check what they have written. They may make some changes to the text or perhaps the layout of the text.

2. Which of the sentences below are in the right register for a blog on global issues? Tick your answer.

   a. I'm pleased about the new computer suite in the school because it is so important for us to keep in touch with events happening around the world.

   b. I find it is an important issue which we will have to deal with at a later date and I will be conducting a survey in the meantime to canvas opinion on the matter.

   c. It is so cool we are having lessons on global issues next term. After all, these issues will affect our future.

Looking closely

You will need to check several things while you are writing your blog, including these:

- Content – will the content interest your reader?

- Register – have you used the correct register?

- Relative clauses – have you used the right relative pronouns?

- Facts – have the facts you are using been checked for accuracy?

- Length – blogs must be long enough to contain interesting detail but not so long that the reader leaves without finishing.

3. Before posting this blog, the blogger has asked you to check it. Find and correct five mistakes in the blog.

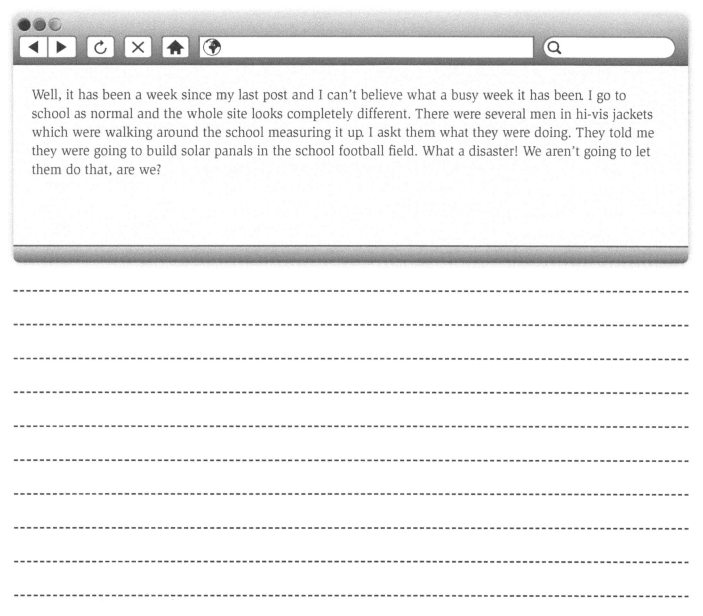

Well, it has been a week since my last post and I can't believe what a busy week it has been. I go to school as normal and the whole site looks completely different. There were several men in hi-vis jackets which were walking around the school measuring it up. I askt them what they were doing. They told me they were going to build solar panals in the school football field. What a disaster! We aren't going to let them do that, are we?

Your blog

Planning

You are going to create a blog focused on a global issue or an aspect of a global issue. It might be an issue you find interesting or one that concerns you.

1. Pick a global issue from the list below that you would like to write about on your blog. Tick your choice.

Recycling	☐	Global economy	☐
Reusable energy	☐	Endangered animals	☐
Growing cities	☐	Life beyond Earth	☐

2. Now you need to think about what you are going to write in your blog. What aspect of your chosen global issue is particularly important at the moment and why? Here are some ideas to help – you can start with one of these and move on to your own ideas later.

    - Recycling plastics and other things which have not been recycled in the past.

    - Having solar panels or a mini windmill at an individual's home; or several all together in a town to supply electricity for the town.

    - The need to build more houses and flats as the population increases in towns, cities and the world generally.

    - The increasing dependence of each country's economy on all the others.

    - The destruction of natural habitats which in turn endangers animals.

    - Whether we will remain living on the Earth or whether we will, in the future, live on other planets, to ease congestion in our cities and to ease the pressure on the resources.

    a. Write down the idea from above that you want to focus on.

    ----

    b. Your blog will be one paragraph long. Now you have your topic, you need one or two facts. Research some facts and then check they are accurate – was the original source reliable? Write your two facts below.

    i.   ---
    ii. ---

    c. You also want to use a relative clause. Write a sentence using either a defining or non-defining relative clause based on one of the facts you have checked.

Teacher tip

A post on a blog will usually cover just one main theme so avoid using several ideas in one go.

A blog needs to be informal. You will usually be addressing your peers – people the same age as you, who may have similar views to your own – so it will be like talking to friends.

A blog needs facts and information, but also explanation. While writing explanations you can use your relative pronouns. There might also be clarifications, for which you can also use relative pronouns.

3. What is the one idea in your blog?

---

4. Write three brief phrases you could include in writing to your friends. Here is an example to get you started:

- *So guys, here is what I think:*

a. ---

b. ---

c. ---

5. Pick out one fact you will use in your blog and add a relative clause, either to explain or to clarify.

Writing

6. Using your plans, on a separate sheet of paper write a post for your blog on a global issue that interests or concerns you. Write 120–180 words. You can choose one of the ideas above or write your own ideas.

Skills checklist

When you have finished your blog, complete the following checklist.

? Have you read about and understood global issues? ☐

? Have you understood how to choose different types of sentence? ☐

? Have you understood and used figurative language? ☐

? Have you understood and used different types of relative clauses? ☐

? Have you written a clear blog? ☐

Checking your progress

1. Ian Somerhalder said, "Millenials don't just want to read the news. They want to know what they can do about it." A millennial is someone who was born after the year 2000. Write your own quote about a global issue you are concerned about and what, as a millenial, you can do about it.

Grammar

2. Draw lines to match each sentence to the correct sentence type.

a. Where are my shoes?	i. Statement
b. Should you being doing that?	ii. Question
c. I should be on the train now.	iii. Rhetorical question
d. Go and pick those books up now.	iv. Command

3. Which of these sentences has used a relative pronoun correctly? Tick your answer.

   a. The boy whose shoes were left on the field usually remembers everything.

   b. The local man which is a dentist does voluntary work for the homeless.

4. Add a relative pronoun to the following sentence.

   • The manager _____ had been working on the renewable energy project for three years.

5. Explain what is meant by the figurative phrase in the sentence below.

   • The new eco-company was being weighed down by paperwork.

Writing

6. Think of an example of a global issues topic not covered in this chapter that you might want to write about on your blog.

---

7. Write two features you would include in this blog to help engage the reader.

a. --

b. --

8. When discussing your ideas for a blog with two friends, they tell you they have written thousands of blogs. How many might they have written and why do you think that?

----

9. Which global issue would you like to learn more about and why?

----

10. a. Which skill have you improved the most in this chapter? Which skill has improved the least? Below is a reminder list of what you have covered. Tick the most improved and put a cross against the least improved.

Types of sentence ☐

Relative clauses ☐

Figurative language ☐

Informal language ☐

Writing a blog ☐

b. Which statement best describes you? Circle your response.

- I know what a blog is, but find it difficult to use the appropriate register. ☐

- I recognise the key elements used in a blog, but find it hard to incorporate them all. ☐

- I'm confident that I can use my knowledge and skills to write an interesting blog. ☐

c. Write a question to ask a friend about a skill they have enjoyed learning. What would you like to know?

Index